Hardcore Self-Defense

Hardcore Self-Defense

C. R. Jahn

Writers Club Press
San Jose New York Lincoln Shanghai

Hardcore Self-Defense

Writers Club Press
an imprint of iUniverse, Inc.

For information address:
iUniverse, Inc.
5220 S. 16th St., Suite 200
Lincoln, NE 68512
www.iuniverse.com

This work is not to be construed as a "training manual!" The techniques and tactics enumerated herein are simply intended to inform and entertain, and are meant for reference purposes only! It would be extremely dangerous, as well as potentially unlawful, to attempt to actually implement many of these techniques, and you are strongly urged to seek alternatives to violence whenever feasible! Remember, "Knowledge is power," yet the true warrior exercises restraint!

ISBN: 0-595-21651-X

To those who have fallen...

Excellent
Book

Contents

Introduction

Welcome! This is guaranteed to be unlike any other "self-defense" manual you've ever read. It is text only, with neither photographs or illustrations, but clearly presents the subject matter in an easily understood format nonetheless. Foreign phrases and specialized jargon have not been utilized, and certain questionable or highly esoteric concepts (like *dim mak*) are not discussed. The material in this volume can easily be applied by anyone of average intelligence (and fitness) with a minimum of practice. No prior martial arts training is required. These concepts will be useful to novices as well as advanced students. You will not be disappointed.

A large portion of *Hardcore Self-Defense* focuses primarily upon psychology. If an individual is not mentally prepared for the possibility of defending oneself against a determined vicious attack, then that individual will probably fail—even if they have studied martial arts or have a weapon on their person! Being attacked is extremely stressful, and if you don't know exactly how to react, you might hesitate an instant too long—or might even *panic* as a result of the adrenaline flooding into your system. In such a situation, psychological strength (confidence, courage, ferocity, willpower, etc.) is far more important than physical strength. If you lack the Combat Mindset, you will be at a huge disadvantage in a physical altercation, and will not be able to properly focus all of your energies on survival. The essays within this volume will provide you with the blueprints you need for transformation.

Hardcore Self-Defense also discusses the various aspects of "Hand-to-Hand" Combat. If you are suddenly required to protect yourself from a violent attacker bent on inflicting serious physical harm to your person, and do not have immediate access to a firearm, you'll need to have a clear understanding of tactics and techniques if you hope to prevail.

1

Simply swinging one's fist, or brandishing one's blade, may not be adequate. This text will also assist you in selecting your primary weapon. It will discuss the strengths, weaknesses, and idiosyncrasies of various weapon types—as well as how they are best implemented for maximum efficiency.

After reading the essays within this volume, you'll be able to maximize your lethal potential, and will have a much greater understanding of what is sometimes required in order to survive. This text is, most definitely, **NOT FOR THE MEEK!**

The first essay in this compilation, entitled *Mental Preparation*, will reveal a number of "mind games" designed to reprogram your brain via self-hypnosis, enabling you to attain the "combat mindset." The second essay, entitled *Invulnerability*, will detail how you can protect yourself from serious threats through the use of inconspicuous armor as well as hypervigilance. *Rape Prevention* will teach you how to walk away from an attempted sexual assault with your attacker's pecker in your pocket. *Unarmed Combat* will discuss various methods of engaging an enemy in weaponless combat—from simple evasion, to brutally effective counter-attacks. *Invisible Weapons* will introduce the student to the concept of improvised weaponry. *Beltfighting* will detail the various ways one's belt may be used to inflict injury upon an aggressor. *Introduction to Knifefighting* contains more useful information than most books devoted entirely to the subject. *Handguns* will discuss the topics of safety, selection, stopping power, concealment, and legalities—as well as provide a number of tips on effective gunfighting. *Primitive Weapons for Home Defense* will discuss the best options available to those warriors who cannot—or choose not to—own a firearm. *Choose Your Weapons!* is a massive compendium of possible weapon types (and subtypes), categorized both by perceived effectiveness (a letter grade of "A" through "F") as well as group classification. And the final essay, entitled *The Aftermath* (which is intended for entertainment purposes only), will tell you how to dispose of your attacker's dead body.

Even expert martial artists will learn something new from the material herein. Read on—I'm quite sure you'll be pleased.

Mental Preparation

INTRODUCTION:

90% of one's combat effectiveness is pre-determined by an individual's mindset. If you are not mentally prepared for the possibility that you might actually need to someday use those martial-arts moves you've been practicing, the value of your strength and skill will be greatly diminished. A naive person with a timid demeanor can easily be victimized by others, regardless of whether he is an athlete or a karate student. *"A sword is useless in the hands of a coward."*

Before any of this can be absorbed, you first must understand that you have both a *right* and a *responsibility* to protect yourself from unlawful attack. If you have certain insecurities or mental blocks, it is necessary that they are overcome before you can proceed. If you are a pacifist or are terrified of possibly breaking the law, you will need to fully address these issues before you will have any chance of successfully defending yourself. If certain misconceptions may prevent you from forcefully reacting to a potentially deadly situation, it is necessary that these misconceptions be cleared up through research and contemplation. No-one has the right to wrongfully threaten or injure another person, and if someone attempts to do so to you, it is permissible (as well as encouraged) that you put an immediate stop to it.

It is important to be strong mentally. If you are easily cowed by aggressive persons, or overly impressed by a muscular physique, you will be an easy target regardless of your level of martial arts training. You need to be able to stand up for yourself, because no-one else will do it for you. If you lack the intestinal fortitude to risk potentially serious injury by engaging an aggressor in unarmed combat, at the very least you can expect to be slapped around and humiliated. Too many traditional martial artists are hesitant to "use their skills" in anything but a true life or death scenario—this is a weakness which can easily be exploited. It is important to realize that, not only does no-one have the right to wrongfully place their hands upon you (even if they apparently do not intend to inflict injury), but your untried "deadly strikes" probably will be a lot less effective than you initially believed (one-strike knockouts are a rarity). Remember, your greatest opponent *lies within*. Once you have overcome your worries, doubts, and fears, you will be a far more formidable fighter.

BASIC CONCEPTS:

Expect to be hurt. The reason many black belts have gotten stomped in streetfights is because they believed themselves to be "invincible." Most martial arts schools *do not* engage in full contact sparring (usually "insurance" reasons are cited, but the sorry truth is that many students would soon stop attending classes after accumulating enough contusions), and those that *do* tend to spar infrequently—and with full protective padding! The average black belt is a pampered athletic wussy with a grossly inflated self-image—when he receives his first broken nose, he may very well be too *shocked* to react! Consider also that the average streetfighter *will not* "square off" so as to "trade punches" within the parameters of a sport karate competition. This will not happen...instead, he'll probably jump on your back, grabbing a fistful of hair with one hand while he pummels your face with the roll of nickels he had stuffed in his pocket for just such an occasion! All those karate magazines that show martial artists flaunting their skills versus mannequin-like opponents have absolutely no basis in reality. Even if you win, you'll probably be fairly well marked up for your troubles. The hero walks away without a scratch only on television.

Identify vulnerable targets as well as strong points. How motivated does he appear to be? Does he seem to be physically powerful? What degree of fighting skill do you think he possesses? Does he appear to be familiar with violence? Can his emotional state be exploited? Does he appear to be intoxicated? How do you think he'll he react to a feint? These questions can often be accurately answered through skillful observation of your opponent's poise and mannerisms. His eyes will tell you a great deal about his level of resolve, and his choice of garb may give you certain insights into his character. A skilled observer can compile a fairly accurate assessment of any given individual (attitude, energy level, profession, social class, self-image, emotional stability, gang affiliation, etc.) within a few moments.

Fear is an important survival tool, because it warns us to exercise caution in the face of danger; however, uncontrolled fear can result in either hysteria or paralysis. Courage is simply doing what needs to be done, regardless of one's fear—it is usually a result of accepting that a risk must be taken (or a sacrifice made) in order to attain one's goal. By allowing yourself to become either highly focused or somewhat detached, it is possible to temporarily banish fear. Think of fear as adrenaline. Truly fearless people are extremely rare—they tend to be robotic sociopaths who, having no hope of future happiness, simply *do not care* what happens to them. Most foolhardy idiots who appear "fearless" are either drunk or trying to impress others.

Think like a machine. This means that one should rely upon logic and eliminate emotion—simply do what needs to be done without thinking about it. It often helps to look at the situation abstractly, pretending that one is an actor in a movie. Emotions can be detrimental to one's goal, and are best shut off for the duration of the crisis. Many emergency workers tend to develop an emotionally detached "working persona" which will remain calm and collected in the face of extreme stress.

If you are faced with overwhelming odds, and for whatever reason are unable to make peace or escape, you must be able to calmly realize that you will probably be killed. Accepting your imminent demise, you then decide to maim and kill as many of your enemies as possible before being beaten into unconsciousness. This can be looked upon as "valor" or it can be seen as retribution for their murdering you. If they see that you are unafraid of death, and are ready to tear into them like a cornered wolverine, they may very well reconsider their actions (especially if they simply like to bully others for amusement purposes)—if not, then at least you'll die valiantly in battle (an end most warriors would be content with).

Once the proper combat mindset is achieved, several benefits will be immediately evident:

1. You will be highly motivated to defend yourself and inflict injury upon your opponent.

2. You will experience an eerie serenity due to the fact that all your emotions have been temporarily shut down, giving you the demeanor of a sociopath.

3. You will experience little pain and no fear. If you sustain a serious, or even a mortal injury, you will continue to fight. Furthermore, you will be utterly unconcerned with any pain or fear felt by your adversary.

4. You will react instantly and perform with ruthless efficiency. You will continue to fight until either the threat is gone or your body is incapable of further action.

With regular training, it will become possible to enter this state instantly, much like the act of flicking a switch. Suddenly, one's face becomes blank, one's eyes become glazed, and one becomes quite disconcerting to confront. Many aggressors would reconsider further action after looking at your face and speculating upon what type of person they might be in close proximity to. Being able to attain the combat mindset is the prerequisite for further study...without it, one can never achieve his full potential as a fighter.

ADVANCED CONCEPTS:

What I am about to share with you is considered by many to be "secret knowledge." It may seem confusing, fanciful, or even stupid—*but it works!* This section will provide an introduction to various unconventional, eclectic, and powerful methods of transforming yourself into a person capable of achieving seemingly impossible goals (such as conquering fear and ignoring pain). You may doubt the veracity of these claims—and it is good to be skeptical—but it is even more important to keep an open mind and judge the facts for yourself, rather than summarily dismissing them due to your preconceptions.

These techniques consist primarily of utilizing visualization and self-hypnosis as tools to focus the will. There is nothing unsavory or "mystical" about these methods, although similar techniques have been used (to great effect) by salesmen and gurus for unscrupulous ends. Due to the fact that various "mind control" techniques can be used to influence others, their use is not without controversy. Even various "self-help" programs relying upon similar methods can take on eerie "cult-like" proportions. It is usually considered unethical (and rightfully so) to subtly manipulate others, whereas there is nothing malevolent about using these methods to heal and strengthen oneself. If you have a weakness, bad habit, or character flaw which is interfering with your life and making you unhappy, then you have a right (as well as a responsibility) to correct it.

REPROGRAMMING:

The first premise you need to understand, is that man's brain is similar in many ways to a computer. A computer is programmed with a variety of software in order to enable it to perform various functions. Different versions (or modifications) of the computer's basic software can customize it to better meet the needs of individual users. The computer's functions are a direct result of its programming. Conversely, man is also "programmed" with a variety of thoughts, ideas, and beliefs. This "programming" consists of personal observations and experiences, combined with what one is taught by others (parents, school, church, television, literature, etc.). One's "programming" begins at infancy, and continues through one's formative years.

Although many people continue to learn, change, and evolve throughout their lives, most people's growth comes to an unfortunate halt shortly after entering the workforce. The goal of self-actualization is difficult to attain when one is drained of energy by toiling at a demeaning job, day after miserable day, in order to pay one's bills. After a long day of tedious and unrewarding labor, the average individual wants to accomplish little more than eat dinner, "unwind" by sitting in front of the television for a few hours (perhaps while drinking a few beers), and then go to bed in order to recharge enough for another day of work. The average man is far too complacent and despondent to exert any effort towards self-improvement, and will tend to ridicule those who do. You are advised not to discuss these matters with those who would distract you through their unwarranted criticism.

Understand that many of the thoughts in your head *are not your own*. They have been placed there by others. Sometimes these imprints are deliberate (religious dogma, scholastic regimentation, propaganda), due to the fact that they are used as "control mechanisms" by the imprinter. However, many times the imprinting is unintentional or co-incidental (fictional entertainment, hearsay, unfounded speculation), and may even occur on a subconscious level. After a lifetime of being inundated with facts, half-truths, and utter falsehoods, one's memory banks are filled with an abundance of useless (or even potentially harmful) data. A good example of this would be the annoying "jingles" which many advertisers use to market their products—in hopes that it will play over and over in your head (like a "loop tape" or computer virus), and influence your next purchase. Indeed, many consumers hum their programmed tunes and parrot inane "catchphrases" as they walk down the supermarket aisles, filling their shopping carts. Identifying "files" which need to be "deleted" is not that difficult, once one realizes that such files exist.

After one has deleted a significant amount of useless garbage, one can then begin to add new programming. First, one must contemplate what one wishes to achieve. Do you require more confidence, courage, or discipline? Start by setting specific goals (like better organizing one's paperwork, or resolving to stick to a regular exercise regimen), then figure out what steps you will need to take before the goal can be achieved. What barriers are preventing you from achieving your goal? If a bad habit (like procrastination) is interfering, you will need to recognize it and take steps to eliminate it. Silly as it may sound, you may find it helpful to post a note with your goal by the mirror, and read it aloud each morning until it has been achieved. Such "statements of intent" (often referred to as "affirmations") have proven to yield excellent results. Realize that it *is* possible to remake yourself into the person you most want to be—then take steps to do so.

PSEUDOSPECIATION:

If it becomes necessary that you must injure, maim, or kill your opponent, it will become much easier to do so once he has become sufficiently dehumanized. In wartime, soldiers are taught that their adversaries are inferior on a biological level (and are often inundated with terminology intended to denigrate the adversaries' race, religion, and culture). While this may seem horribly inappropriate—even monstrous—it has proven to be a powerful psychological tool.

Once you can identify the "other" as, not only "different from us," but as some sort of alien species both beyond our comprehension and below contempt, they suddenly become surprisingly easy (even desirable) to kill. During wartime, this is considered to be a good thing (studies have shown that soldiers lacking such indoctrination have a tendency to either fire their weapons well over their enemies, or simply not fire their weapons at all).

There are many ways that this can be done. First, a long list of inhuman atrocities, allegedly committed by the opponents versus defenseless civilians and prisoners of war, is revealed. Then, the opponents are referred to abstractly as "targets," "enemies," or "aggressors." Finally, the soldiers are encouraged to ridicule everything about the opponents, using derogatory slurs to do so. Once the opponent has been sufficiently demonized, the soldiers will truly believe that all persons within the opponent's demographic should be wiped out for the good of humanity.

Contrary to what their public relations officers might have us believe, law enforcement personnel make frequent use of pseudospeciation. In the academy, rookies are taught about the differences between "us" and "them," and this mindset is cultivated and encouraged to flourish once he begins working with experienced street cops (who have significantly fewer restrictions upon what they are permitted to instruct). Common unofficial terms for lawbreaking types include: degenerate, scumbag, dirtbag, creature, beast, and skell. Such dehumanization promotes brutality and other abuses of power, and serves as justification for the "wall of silence" response to allegations of misconduct.

By thinking abstractly, and identifying your opponent as something "subhuman" (for example: a goblin, troll, zombie, or caveman), it is possible to achieve a killer mindset in short order. By visualizing such a loathsome creature standing before you, you will automatically expect to be lied to and misdirected prior to your attempted victimization, so it is highly unlikely that you will be tricked or surprised. Furthermore, you will not hesitate to respond to a perceived threat, and you will strive to inflict maximum damage forthwith. If, instead, one were to misidentify one's opponent as "a fellow human being in distress," it would be much more difficult to respond quickly and appropriately to a sudden attack. How you view your opponent will greatly influence your reaction to his provocations.

VISUALIZATION:

Many successful athletes and entrepreneurs began by visualizing themselves achieving their goals. They did this repeatedly, with great clarity, in effect creating a movie within their minds which they could review over and over again, inspiring them towards greatness (even though others may have dismissed their dreams as unrealistic). Eventually, many of them achieve their goal. This is because, not only did they never lose sight of it, but they could not conceive of failure—if they had a setback, they would begin anew, *but they would never give up!* The martial artist can use this powerful tool to great personal advantage.

Great personal power can be achieved through several steps. Although they may seem simplistic at first, when used correctly they have the ability to transform you. Each step should be taken in order, and if you intend to do this properly, you should expect to spend at least several hours (which can be split up into half-hour meditation sessions) on each step before proceeding to the next. Be advised—your imagination is a very powerful thing, and it is possible to experience strong emotions or even an adverse reaction (especially if you've had past traumatic experiences), so use discretion when undertaking these exercises. If they make you too uncomfortable, or if they "don't seem to be working," feel free to skip this section altogether.

1. Why would I fight? Under what circumstances would I avoid fighting?

2. Under what circumstances would I be morally justified in killing?

3. Visualize fighting an opponent (unarmed, armed, or multiple).

4. Visualize being beaten & victimized.

5. Visualize being helpless as you are stomped, tortured, or raped.

6. Visualize your death, transport to the morgue, and eventual disposal.

7. Visualize killing your attacker(s).

8. Visualize yourself as powerful.

If done correctly, this series of visualizations will eliminate any hesitation you might have about using violence versus an aggressor. It will also enable you to rationally and maturely consider the consequences of fighting, as well as also enabling you to come to terms with the concept of your eventual demise.

DETACHMENT:

By looking at yourself and your opponent abstractly, it is possible to inflict and sustain grievous physical harm without experiencing panic or revulsion. This is best accomplished by looking at the human body as a machine. If the internal structure of the machine is cracked, that part of the machine will suffer impaired function. If the exterior of the machine is torn or punctured, essential fluids will leak out. If an optic receptor is damaged, the other is still usable. This may seem like a bizarre concept, but by visualizing your body as a giant robot, with a control room within the brainpan where the consciousness is securely strapped into a chair (equipped with joysticks and pedals) before a bank of viewscreens and gauges, it is possible to lose a limb or sustain a potentially mortal wound without panicking (and thus becoming illogical and inefficient). If you can visualize yourself as such, you will succeed in disassociating yourself with your body, which can result in a reduction of felt pain as well as a substantial increase in willpower.

The Navy SEALS refer to something similar, which they call "the porthole effect," in which one's body is like a vehicle, and one is peering out at the world through a pair of portholes (Delta Force troops refer to this state as "the drone zone")—this is commonly experienced by those exhausted troops who've made it to the final week of BUD/S training through sheer willpower. People who have been physically drained, subject to starvation, brutalized by prison guards, mauled by bears or sharks, horrendously injured in a variety of ways, or forcibly raped have often reported entering this state, in which it seems like everything is happening to someone else—perhaps an actor on a movie screen. In extreme instances, some people have even reported that they had *physically separated from their body* and were actually viewing themselves from above! While these reports cannot be substantiated, the fact remains that if one can succeed in intellectually detaching oneself from one's body, one will be able to withstand levels of stress, pain, and fear that most others would find intolerable.

THE MOVIE:

This is a difficult concept for many people to grasp, but it is one of the most powerful methods of self-improvement we know of. It has its basis in certain occult teachings, but there is no "magic" involved—except for the results. In the original teachings, one is told about the many invisible beings which we encounter every day, and how people who lead interesting lives tend to attract these beings, which may even feel compelled to intervene on our behalf in time of need. Positive behavior attracts positive beings, and negative behavior attracts negative beings. We thought that this was an interesting concept, but decided to alter it in order to make it more suitable for defensive applications. Simply think of yourself as the protagonist in an ongoing movie about your life. The movie is put on hold while you're sleeping (except for the occasional interesting "dream sequence"), but is being viewed by an unseen audience at all other times—until shortly after your eventual demise. Your control over the script is limited primarily to the dialogue and actions of your character. You will decide how he (you) reacts to various crisis situations—will he proceed calmly and bravely, or will he instead scream like a girl and run away? The choice is yours—and the audience is watching. Is your character interesting, or is he boring? Is he likable, or is he despicable? Will your story be an adventure, a drama, a comedy, a tragedy, a romance, a combination of the above, or something altogether different? If you do not like your character, feel free to transform him into something more suitable for your purposes. Make sure your character always is presentable in appearance, and conducts himself in a proper manner—even when he thinks no-one's looking. Always try to do the right thing, proceed with valor, and don't behave like an idiot (through giving in to: rage, pettiness, dishonesty, lechery, or other forms of immaturity). Above all, *don't bore your audience!* No-one wants to waste their time watching some pathetic, stoop-shouldered, procrastinating, slothful, wage-slave mope! Don't be afraid to do what you want, stand up for yourself, and live up to your full potential…after all, *it's only a movie!*

THE COMBAT MINDSET:

You have read through these pages and done your best to understand the concepts herein. Now, you suddenly find yourself confronted by an unknown belligerent aggressor. The circumstances of the confrontation are relatively unimportant, as is a detailed description of the aggressor's appearance. Let us simply say that the aggressor in this example is much larger than yourself, apparently unarmed, and seems intent upon using his size and anger to intimidate you into submission before smacking you around for his amusement. Are you afraid? Most people surely would be, but not you. Yes, you are aware of his size and potential strength, and are aware that you would probably be injured in a physical confrontation, but you are not most people. The aggressor is puzzled—you are not sniveling and groveling, nor are you retreating. Instead, you stare fixedly into his eyes, your face expressionless. The goblin stands before you, and he's a big one. For whatever reason, you have determined that retreat is not an option in this situation. Everybody dies eventually, and it is better to die valiantly in combat than to die a "straw death" in one's sickbed at an advanced age. In this situation, for reasons of your own, you would rather die than retreat—and you'll never give up. You are familiar with death, and have come to terms with the concept of your own eventual death long ago—it is important to die well. You look up at your viewscreen and analyze the goblin for weaknesses. The creature's eyes and throat are vulnerable, and would be within easy reach after taking a single step. The knee could be blown out with a side kick. Its fat gut could be laid open with a slash of the serrated utility knife clipped to the inside of your front pants pocket. You could draw your belt and beat it senseless with the heavy pewter buckle, or you could simply pick something up off the table and bounce it off the goblin's head. The goblin's leering face will be your primary target. A digitalized crosshairs appears on the viewscreen…target acquired. Satisfied, you allow a faint smile to cross your face. The goblin suddenly falters and looks away. It mutters a final insult before retreating. It looked into your eyes and knew it was outmatched. The audience cheers.

Invulnerability

invulnerable adj: incapable of being wounded, injured, or harmed

Anyone with a modicum of common sense realizes that true invulnerability is an impossible goal. If a group of enemies wants you dead, has the resources to achieve this goal, and truly does not care how many casualties they take in the process, your best chance of survival would simply be to *disappear*. If, however, self-imposed exile is not an option, certain steps may be taken to slightly increase the odds in your favor.

I am assuming that the reader is physically fit, reasonably skilled at unarmed combat, has access to weapons, and has both understood and applied the concepts of awareness (enumerated in the three books on our "Required Reading" list). If this statement does *not* apply to you, you'll need to work on the basics before making any attempt to study advanced concepts.

In this section, the two primary elements of "invulnerability" shall be addressed: armor and hypervigilance.

ARMOR:

The concept of wearing "armor" may seem rather bizarre to someone from contemporary civilized society, but a warrior will quickly grasp the value of protective gear. Armor comes in many forms, and may be utilized to reduce the risk of serious injury associated with certain specific types of attack.

Most people are familiar with "bulletproof" vests—which are commonly referred to as "body armor." These typically consist of thick Kevlar pads (woven from many layers of ballistic nylon) slid into large pockets on the front and back of a thin nylon vest. Better quality vests may also incorporate smaller side panels, as well as a steel (or ceramic) "trauma plate" worn over the sternum. Other materials (such as Spectrashield) are similar to Kevlar, yet thinner and lighter (however, they are also far more expensive). These vests are typically bulky, hot, and uncomfortable. They will stop most handgun and shotgun ammunition (although the impact can still result in bruises and fractures), but will not stop a tiny hyper-velocity .22 magnum projectile, nor the rounds from most hunting rifles. SWAT teams and elite military personnel have access to special ceramic body armor which will stop rounds from 30.06 and .308 rifles, but such vests are extremely expensive and can weigh over 50 pounds.

What many folks do not realize is that a few manufacturers offer lines of fashionable clothing (from leather jackets to 3-piece suits—and they even have kid's sizes!) impregnated with bullet-resistant fibers. These items are very costly, but they are more comfortable and less conspicuous than a vest. Bullet-resistant items, such as briefcases, umbrellas, and clipboards, are also available. Most distributors of body armor will also sell just the bullet-resistant inserts (in a variety of sizes), which one can affix within one's own jacket at a greatly reduced price.

A heavy leather jacket will prove highly effective versus most knife attacks, and can even deflect low velocity bullets (such as the .25 ACP, .32 ACP, .32 Long, and .38 Special)…just make sure to zip up the front! In warmer weather, a thick leather vest will protect one's torso.

A heavy work jacket made of wool, canvas, or flannel-lined denim can also be counted on to protect oneself from being slashed, and will even provide limited protection versus stabs and gunshots. If confronted with a skilled knifefighter or an attack dog, one would be advised to partially remove one's jacket to wrap it tightly around one's weak arm, to serve as a shield or a "tease." If you are not wearing a jacket, a sweatshirt or towel could also be wrapped in this manner.

Bracers (often incorrectly referred to as "gauntlets") are a protective leather covering of the wrist or forearm. They can be held in place with buckles or snaps—low quality costume bracers are simply laced up, leaving the vulnerable tendons and blood vessels virtually unprotected. Punk rockers, metalheads, and S&M freaks like to play dress-up with bracers covered with chrome-plated studs, spikes, or bondage rings, but these additions just draw attention to yourself and will probably make you look foolish. Plain leather bracers (with possibly a couple antiqued conchos or brass studs, if you require some sort of decoration) are great for protecting your wrists from being cut (possibly rendering that hand useless), and can even be used to block attacks from light bludgeons (like broomsticks and pool-cues). If you wish to maintain a low profile, they can even be hidden under long sleeves. Bracers made from Kevlar can be obtained from various suppliers of law-enforcement paraphernalia.

Gauntlets are heavy-duty protective gloves which cover the wrist. Rawhide work gloves or leather motorcycle gauntlets will both serve well to protect one's hands from being cut—it will even be possible to actually grab an enemy's blade! Gloves made from Kevlar (Wizard Gloves) or fine steel mesh can be obtained from meatcutting suppliers. A gauntlet is best worn in conjunction with a bracer on one's weak hand, leaving the dominant hand bare to better draw one's weapon without fumbling.

A kidney belt, weight-lifting belt, or back-brace can be worn to protect the kidneys from a fatal knife thrust to the renal artery (one of the most common "quick-kill" targets), if a leather jacket or vest cannot be worn. Some of these belts will also cover the bladder and lower solar plexus area.

A wool turtleneck sweater, knit scarf, or decorative bone and bead choker can all offer limited protection versus a power-slash to the carotid artery (another common lethal attack). Just don't wear your collar up like Elvis, or people will think you're a dumbass. Such covering will *not*, however, offer any significant protection versus a crushing blow to the windpipe.

Various forms of eye protection (wraparound shades, prescription glasses with elastic strap, athletic eye protectors, and goggles) will offer different levels of protection versus finger gouges, thrown debris, broken glass, and even (to a limited degree) pepperspray (which is commonly found in the possession of criminals and other troublemakers).

A groin cup is a worthwhile investment if your occupation or lifestyle regularly results in physical altercations. The groin is a favored target area, due to the likelihood of resultant incapacitation without risk of death (and many attack dogs also favor the groin), so wearing a cup can help keep you out of the hospital with ruptured gonads.

A motorcycle helmet can offer good protection versus bludgeoning, thrown objects, and low velocity gunfire. Held by the chinstrap, can also be transformed into a devastating flail.

High boots (engineer, wellington, or cowboy) will prevent a knife-fighter from slicing your Achilles tendon (a nasty surprise attack), and will offer limited protection versus kicks to the shins, ankle-biting dogs, and venomous snakes. Furthermore, the heels and toes of such sturdy footwear provide one with formidable weaponry. Thin leather patches sewn inside the backs of the legs on a pair of loose jeans can offer some protection versus being hamstrung.

A hinged knee-brace will effectively protect your knee from being blown out by the dreaded low side-kick, but wearing such gear will have a significant effect on one's mobility.

Shields can be improvised from many common objects. A trash can lid can be used to deflect blades, bludgeons, thrown objects, and "mouse-gun" projectiles. If the lid happens to be galvanized steel, the edge can be used to strike with. If the lid is constructed of flexible plastic, it can be used to trap a blade which has been thrust through it. A briefcase, gymbag, purse, clipboard, book, stool, or frying pan can all be transformed into a shield in short order—most can also be used to strike with.

If you have adequate protection—and are armed as well—you'll have little to fear from most low-level threats.

HYPERVIGILANCE:

When is the best time to kill a man? When he is unprepared and vulnerable. Do you truly believe that you could never be caught off guard? How ready for action do you think you'd be fast asleep at 0400? How deadly would you be standing naked in the shower with shampoo in your eyes? How fearsome would you be sitting on the crapper with your trousers bunched around your ankles? Be honest with yourself.

A man is most vulnerable when he is sleeping. Unless a man is half-awake, and somewhat aware of what is going on around him, it is a simple matter for a rank amateur to sneak up barefoot and saw halfway through his neck with a large kitchen knife. How does one prevent such an occurrence? Through vigilance! Actually, to be more accurate, through the twitchy paranoid state commonly referred to as "hypervigilance."

An alarm system can give one (false) peace of mind, but any experienced burglar can bypass or disable all but the most sophisticated versions. A protection dog can also sound an alarm, but most dogs can easily be dispatched through a variety of insidious methods, or he could simply be having an off day (incidentally, if a target is known to have a dog, many amateur assassins will attempt to poison it several days before embarking on their "mission"). If you live in squalor, perhaps the assassin will trip over something in the dark, or make noise as he steps on old chip bags and wadded up newspapers (just kidding—if your abode is this filthy, you'd probably be too drunk or stoned to wake up anyway). I would advise affixing a bell to your bedroom doorknob, even though it's locked ("keyhole-in-the-knob" locks can be picked by an amateur—with inferior tools—in under 3 minutes; and those pushbutton "privacy locks" can easily be sprung by a kindergartner with a paperclip), as well as any windows you keep open for a breeze—even if you're on the 3rd floor.

The best way to secure your abode (other than locks, alarms, and dogs), is to do a thorough "walk-through" with a handgun and flashlight (even in the daytime) after the house has been unoccupied for an extended duration. First, check all the obvious locations for a psychotic goblin to hide: the basement, the closets, behind the shower curtain, behind the sofa, the storage room, the laundry room, the attic, and under the bed. If you're really worried about the possibility of being attacked by a "ninja freak," you can also check: inside the dirty clothes hamper, inside the clothes dryer, under the sinks, under the desks, inside the cupboards, up the chimney, up in the rafters, or within the dropped ceiling—unless you've studied either criminology or yoga, you'd be astounded at the tiny spaces a small flexible individual can squeeze himself into! I would only advise going this far if you're being stalked and threatened by a freak whom you *know* has gained access to your house in the past. Research has shown that in many cases where an individual had been killed in his sleep by an intruder, the intruder had already been *hiding within the house* when the victim came in the door—sometimes waiting for hours before making his move. If you check all potential hiding places thoroughly, it is highly unlikely that you will ever be killed in your sleep (unless, of course, you delight in tormenting other family members).

The steps taken to ensure one's safety during copulation are very similar to those taken prior to sleep. Signs of unauthorized entry are looked for, and various rooms and hiding places checked prior to disrobing. One's clothing should be easily accessible, as should be a weapon and flashlight. The doors should be locked (with a wedge placed under the bedroom door), and the phone's ringer switched off. Avoid having sex in parks, campgrounds, or beaches which the general public has access to. If you must have sex in a motor vehicle, ascertain that the windows are up (leave one cracked, so you can hear someone approaching the vehicle) and all doors are locked; be sure to leave the keys in the ignition, keep the stereo turned down low (if it's on at all), have immediate access to a revolver and flashlight, and have no lights on other than the illuminated instrument panel. If you choose to have sex in a motel room, be aware that everyone on the maintenance and housekeeping staff (as well as a few of their burglar boyfriends) have masterkeys—wedging a chair under the doorknob (possibly with the legs in a spare pair of shoes to reduce the chance of slippage) can slow them down if they choose to ignore the "Do Not Disturb" sign. Always be suspicious of slutty strangers attempting to lure you into a secluded area for implied (or stated) purposes of sex—there is a high probability that she might be setting you up for a robbery or a hit.

A man is most vulnerable when he is naked and weaponless. This most often happens to be when one is in the shower. If it is a public (or institutional) shower-room, you'll need to be extra cautious, and really ought to have an associate standing guard. A "Soap-on-a-Rope" is invaluable for public showering—not only is it far less likely that you might drop it, but you'll have at the ready a potentially lethal flail. A full toothpaste tube can either be used as a *yawara* (cap end) or an improvised cutter (the sharp corners of the crimped end). A bathtowel can be transformed into several types of improvised weapon as well (whip, blackjack, garotte, trap, or shield). If it is your own bathroom, you can stow a recently oiled stainless-steel derringer in the medicine cabinet (if you are licenced to carry, you could even wear it in an ankle holster in a public shower-room—provided it's a big-bore, for better drainage). Only use a small amount of shampoo to reduce the amount of suds, the time required to rinse, and the likelihood that one might be temporarily blinded (indeed, many convicts wait until they are safely locked within their own cell before washing their hair). If you are in your own bathroom, a showerhead affixed to a hose, the shower-curtain-rod, and the toilet-tank-lid can all be used as emergency weapons.

When answering the "call of nature," one must be aware that one is extremely vulnerable—especially if one must conduct one's business in a public lavatory. An average man standing exposed in front of a urinal, with both hands on his pecker and his back to the room, can be successfully mugged by a belligerent twelve-year-old. It is recommended that one urinate, instead, within a locked toilet stall. The average man might easily go into "brain-lock" and freeze if an assailant chose to break the social taboo on interpersonal contact whilst urinating. A warrior, however, would not hesitate to draw his weapon—without even interrupting his piss!

If one must sit upon the commode, it is recommended that one place one's handgun, pepperfoam, or blade either in one's lap or in the basket formed by one's underwear betwixt one's knees. If you are in your own bathroom (with the door locked, of course) and haven't a proper weapon, a full aerosol can of disinfectant spray works surprisingly well. One's belt makes a fine improvised flail, and in close quarters could be wrapped up to blackjack size. In a worst case scenario, the plunger's handle could be brought into service as a bludgeon (although the thin lightweight stick would be far more effective to jab with).

If you find yourself in a "weapon-free" environment (such as a school, hospital, or beach), any weapon you choose to carry must be small and concealable. A "neck- knife" could be worn under one's shirt, or a derringer could be secreted in a truss rig (crotch holster). If one must pass through a magnetometer, one could either pack a non-ferrous blade (titanium, ceramic, or fiberglass) or simply rely upon one's belt or keys (swung from a lanyard or tasseled fob). If one must go into a hot tub or sauna, one's stainless-steel derringer could be secreted within a towel. In the unlikely event that one must inconspicuously walk through a nudist colony, one could sew a holster within one's hat. Keister guns, like the "Stinger," would only be considered by a deep-cover assassin or a latent homosexual.

In the unfortunate event that one finds oneself incarcerated in either a correctional or mental health facility, weapons can still be fabricated from one's environment. Bedsprings can be sharpened into shanks by repeatedly rubbing them against the concrete floor to shape and sharpen. Televison and radio antennaes, as well as toothbrush handles, can be similarly fashioned into much flimsier weapons. A sharpened pencil makes an excellent single-use shank—be sure to carry several. A disposable ballpoint pen can serve as a pointy *yawara*-type weapon, but is unlikely to penetrate deeply. A bar of soap dropped into a tube sock makes an excellent blackjack. A newspaper can be tightly rolled into a stiff tube to jab into the throat and solar plexus, or it can be bent around the knuckles and grasped in the fist to form a set of improvised "knucks." A TV cable or extension cord can be swung like a flail (or whip), used to bind and trap incoming blows, or used to strangle with. Broomsticks, mop wringers, cleaning solvents, flaming shoe polish, sharp pork chop bones, and cigarette ashes can all be used as improvised weapons. If you've been threatened by an enemy, you can tape newspapers or magazines under your shirt to armor your belly and kidneys against shank attacks. If you are expected to sleep in a "dormitory" environment, be sure not to sleep too soundly until you finally have opportunity to kick the shit out of the first idiot to fuck with you, after which you may feel free to relax in the safety of your own cell.

If you are seriously ill, infirm, or recovering from major injuries, a derringer or small automatic could be worn in an ankle-rig. I strongly advise you *not* to consider stowing a weapon under your pillow, as the risk of misplacement or accidental discharge is far too great. If you are suffering from acute nausea or extreme weakness, it will be extremely difficult to defend yourself, so you should post a guard.

As has been stated elsewhere, it is foolish, irresponsible, and dangerous to allow yourself to become shitfaced drunk or whacked out of your gourd on drugs. If you choose to do so, your awareness level, reaction time, and judgement will all be shot. Be sure never to combine alcohol (even half a beer) with sleeping pills, allergy medication, muscle relaxants, or other prescription pharmaceuticals which might have an adverse reaction. Never allow anyone other than a trusted friend to secure a drink for you, and never let your drink out of your sight! Never accept a joint (or even a cigarette) from a stranger, as it could be laced with PCP, LSD, or poison. If you decide to take hallucinogens recreationally, *never* do so in a public place (especially at a concert or festival). Remember, large doses of hallucinogens can render a strong man contemptibly helpless. Don't even *think* about fucking around with opiates! Any drug that can make an individual grin blissfully whilst crapping his britches (or being slapped around) is *not* for the warrior!

Always think ahead. Always be aware of what's going on around you. Trust your intuition. And remember—you're not being "paranoid" if an enemy is truly out to get you!

Rape Prevention

WARNING!

This section contains graphic depictions of extreme violence, as well as other material which may be offensive to some readers. The techniques, as well as the opinions, detailed herein are not suitable for everyone.

NOTE

Believe it or not, much of the information in this section could be useful to a man as well—particularly if he were facing the possibility of long-term incarceration for having rightfully defended himself, or for violation of any one of the hundreds of prosecutable "non-crimes" forbidden by those currently in power. Homosexual rape in correctional institutions is disturbingly commonplace—and the staff members seldom take any action to make these facilities safer.

Many self-defense courses directed at females purport to teach their students "rape prevention." Unfortunately, most of them are inadequate for a variety of reasons, the primary reason being that they do not look at the crime of rape realistically. Through failing to prepare their students with the shock of being faced with a determined vicious attacker intent on rape, and by offering unsuitable defenses that are half- heartedly practiced with complacent partners (often other students), they provide one with little more than a false sense of security. Let us examine the facts.

Rape is a heinous crime—many people consider it to be far worse than murder, and for good reason. A murder victim's pain is soon over, but a victim of rape often suffers for the rest of their life. Such suffering can include, but is by no means limited to: an incurable viral infection, an unwanted pregnancy, post-traumatic stress disorder, flashbacks of the event, paranoia, depression, sleep disorders, anxiety disorders, digestive disorders, and a variety of neuroses and self-destructive behaviors. These problems can seriously impede one's ability to interact socially or enjoy a normal life. Many rape victims are fearful of leaving their house or being left alone. Many rape victims either commit suicide or, through dangerous compulsions (reckless driving, excessive abuse of prescription medications, abuse of illicit drugs, ect.), repeatedly put themselves at risk of being killed. Many rape victims are psychologically devastated by the event, and few are ever able to fully recover, even after many years have passed. Rape destroys lives, and the perpetrators seldom are punished accordingly. You need to be able to fully visualize both the crime and the aftermath before you can even begin to comprehend the magnitude of this offense. Far too many ignorant dolts fail to see rape as an act of unrestrained evil, and tend to downgrade it or even go so far as to blame the victim. Rape is, by far, the worst thing one human can do to another. It is an unforgivable act, and the perpetrators should be eliminated from society.

According to FBI statistics, over 75% of all forcible sex crimes (rape, forcible sodomy, forcible fondling, and other forms of sexual abuse) involved the use of "personal weapons" (hands, fists, feet)—in other words, the offender was *unarmed*, relying simply upon superior physical force (or the threat of injury) to subdue his victim. The lack of an actual weapon *does* give you an added advantage—but surprisingly, it often confounds some self-defense students, who might feel that blinding or castrating an unarmed man is *unjustified*, and thus rely upon simple punches and kicks versus a much larger opponent (which often proves ineffective). According to the law in most jurisdictions, if you feel that you are in imminent danger of being maimed or killed, you are allowed to employ lethal force to protect yourself. If your unarmed attacker is significantly larger than yourself, or is accompanied by others (whether they are active participants or not), you are entitled to take his life in the event of an unprovoked and unlawful assault. A larger attacker can easily crush your throat, gouge your eyes, or stomp your head into a thick red paste if given the opportunity—do not make the mistake of thinking that his lack of a weapon somehow makes him less dangerous!

Rape is loosely defined as "forcible penile penetration of the vagina or anus," but that is not always accurate. A person unable to give consent is considered to have been raped in the event of sexual intercourse. A person is deemed unable to consent if they: are extremely intoxicated, are considered to be mentally incompetent due to mental illness, are retarded, or are a child or minor. A person who is coerced into having sex by an implied threat of violence also is considered to have been raped. Sometimes a foreign object is used to penetrate the victim, often resulting in severe injury or death. Contrary to popular belief, men account for approximately 10% of all reported rapes and one third of all gang rapes. In a few atrociously mismanaged correctional facilities, it has been estimated that the average male inmate has about a 75% chance of being gang raped during the first month of his incarceration, and homosexual rape is often used to break the will of POWs held in less civilized countries. Rape is usually often used as a means to proclaim the attacker's dominance through the humiliation of his victim. In cases of incest, rape is used as a means to assert total control over the victim. In seemingly "random" assaults, rape is often committed out of hatred and envy of someone who is seen as being better than the assailant, thus unattainable through normal means. The offender can always find some twisted way to justify his actions to himself and others. Very seldom is rape the simple result of uncontrolled lust. Unlike murder, battery, or even armed robbery, there can never be any plausible explanation to exonerate someone for the crime of forcible rape. "I was drunk and didn't know what I was doing," is the bullshit excuse most often heard. Rape destroys lives, and it has been statistically proven that the overwhelming majority of rapists are repeat offenders incapable of being rehabilitated.

When one is victimized by someone they know, it is often referred to as "date rape" or "acquaintance rape." Many people make the mistake of minimizing such instances as something distinct from "forcible rape." In fact, in the majority of such instances the victim is incapable of consent due to intoxication or having been drugged, and often the victim is further subdued through force or threat of violence. Because alcohol is a factor in most of these cases, one can take precautions by: taking care not to overimbibe, making sure that no-one (especially your "date") has opportunity to tamper with your drink, and observing how your friend handles his alcohol. Intoxication dulls both the awareness and reaction time of a potential victim, as well as emboldens a potential aggressor. Never willingly place yourself in a situation where you would have difficulty protecting yourself.

Most self-defense instructors simply tell women to "kick him in the groin," or "poke him in the eyes with your keys"…both proven to be ineffective techniques versus a serious threat. Others advise you to "scream for help," or even tell women to soil themselves in an attempt to appear less desirable! In the majority of forcible rapes, after initially appearing friendly and non-threatening as a means of taking the victim off guard, the attacker moves closer before surprising the victim with a sudden vicious attack—usually either choking the victim into semi-consciousness or grabbing a handful of clothing while repeatedly slapping the victim hard across the face to stun them into immobility. Once the victim is sufficiently incapacitated, the assault takes place, after which the victim is often killed to prevent them from testifying in court. You will not be able to stop a determined vicious assault with half-assed techniques that would only deter a wussy! You need to inflict maximal damage.

A man with his genitals exposed is extremely vulnerable. The penis and testicles have numerous blood vessels and nerves, as well as soft moorings. Even a relatively weak strike to this area can be temporarily debilitating, though people's pain tolerances vary greatly, and may be dulled by alcohol, drugs, psychosis, or other factors. The male genitals can be bruised, crushed, or torn, resulting in shock, nausea, extreme pain, and massive hemorrhaging. The testicles can be kicked, punched, slapped, squoze, or grasped and yanked sharply—possibly tearing the scrotum or even resulting in castration, although this is unlikely. It is possible, though extremely difficult, to actually rupture the testicles by grasping them and crushing with all one's strength. A flaccid penis can easily be separated from the body if grasped and yanked sharply (at the very least, profuse internal bleeding will result). An erect penis can be pulled forcefully downward to snap tissue and rupture blood vessels, quite possibly resulting in permanent impotence—it can also be crushed, mutilated, or even severed with one's teeth. Any significant vascular or neurological damage to the genitals may very well prove irreparable (the fact that John Wayne Bobbit had immediate access to a skilled microsurgeon—and the additional fact that the operation proved successful—was highly anomalous). That goblin will never rape again if you take away his means of doing so.

Rape ruins lives. You are to avoid being raped through any means necessary. If you are raped, not only will you be humiliated, possibly infected, and emotionally traumatized, but you may very well be murdered to ensure your silence—do not depend on the mercy of the goblins, and never believe anything they tell you! Statistics prove that victims who do not resist their attackers are *just as likely* to be beaten or killed as those who fight back, so what have you got to lose? If you choose not to resist, chances are that you will forever regret it. Even if you are unsuccessful, as long as you fight to the best of your ability and refuse to give up, it will be easier to deal with the aftermath. Chances are that your attacker has done this before and will do it again. If you can gouge out his eye or bite off his nose, you must do so, even if he has a knife to your throat and you think you may be killed as a result—he probably intended to kill you anyway, so your final act must ensure that he won't get away with it! With the proliferation of the fatal HIV/AIDS virus among drug users and convicts, automatically assume that your attacker is infected and capable of transmitting the disease to you (at the very least, you will probably be infected with hepatitis or a STD). Assume that once the act is completed, you will be killed one way or another. Escape through whatever means necessary and, failing that, be completely willing to sacrifice your life in the process of killing your attacker.

A common ploy rapists and serial killers sometimes use is to impersonate a police officer. Often, such offenders may drive a vehicle similar in appearance to an unmarked police car (that may even be equipped with a detachable flashing light, which can be ordered through several mail-order companies by anyone) and flash a counterfeit badge at their intended victim, hoping to lure or intimidate them into a vulnerable position. Such individuals, usually having a perverse affinity for police lingo and paraphernalia, are commonly referred to as "badge freaks." Although policemen *have* occasionally been known to rape or murder women—sometimes even while on duty—such occurrences are extremely rare. As a general rule, never assume an unknown man flashing a badge at you is actually a cop just because he claims to be; if the circumstances seem questionable, or he behaves in an inappropriate manner, prepare to flee or defend yourself. A policeman is not allowed to handcuff someone, order them into their vehicle, or otherwise "take them into custody" without a very good reason, so don't let anyone bullshit you. A badge freak is relying upon a symbol of authority to instil fear, respect, and trust in his victims—a reaction he'd be unable to produce otherwise. If you suspect you've been accosted by a badge freak, immediately drive to a police station or call a *real* cop on your cell phone.

Never submit to threats, and NEVER under any circumstances allow your attacker to isolate you in a vehicle or abandoned building—if he is able to isolate you, he can proceed at his leisure, and your chances of survival will be reduced to nearly zero. Nearly all serial killers either lured or forced their victims into a vehicle (sometimes the victim's own) before incapacitating them (often with a sap, stun gun, pepperspray, or strangulation), binding them (usually with duct tape or handcuffs), and transporting them to a secluded area that had been prepared in advance for the victim's arrival. People have escaped from such situations, but the vast majority do not. If an attacker attempts to isolate you or remove you from the area, his intent is to kill you (although he will probably say otherwise in hopes of gaining your compliance). If you are faced with similar circumstances (the threat of being bound, kidnapped, or choked unconscious) and are unable to immediately escape, your intent must be to kill him. Use whatever improvised weapons are available to you, scream, bite, kick, and gouge. Hit his throat and claw his eyes, but *never give up fighting until you are dead* or the aggressor flees. If he merely disengages and retreats a short distance, he is preparing to attack you again—do not permit him to collect himself! If he has disengaged, it is probably because he was startled or injured and needs a few moments to reassess the situation before focusing on your weak points and wearing you down. If you cannot escape, *KILL!* Transform your paralyzing fear into adrenaline fueled rage! Transform yourself into a vicious animal! Leap at him, get a secure hold on his clothing or hair, and start chewing his face off! Remember, the average Pit Bull only weighs between 65 and 80 pounds—and you know what kind of damage *they* can do! While a human's jaw strength cannot compare to that of a large dog, it is controlled by some of the most powerful muscles in the body. A wholly committed human can easily crush metacarpals and tear off dripping hunks of meat when in the throes of an adrenaline induced "feeding frenzy." Put *him* on the defense. Unless he has a gun in his hand, soon *he* will be the one trying to escape!

Faced with a committed defense, most attackers will abort and flee after trying unsuccessfully to subdue you. They are intent on enjoying themselves at your expense, are dependant on your being stunned into immobility, and will be unwilling to present their vulnerable genitalia to an individual with the characteristics of a cornered wolverine. Expect no mercy, and give no quarter! If you are mentally capable of visualizing every abominable detail of such an attack, as well as its aftermath, this is easily done. If you have no idea what you're in for, you can easily freeze in terror or be duped into believing the goblin when he tells you that you "won't be hurt" if you do as you're told. Pacifists make ideal victims. If you cannot escape, you must be 100% committed to blinding, maiming, or killing your attacker. Not only will this probably distract him enough to allow you to escape, but it will allow him to feel a fraction of the pain and terror he has inflicted upon others throughout his worthless existence. If you cannot do it for yourself, do it on behalf of his past and future victims. Never give up! Don't be a weakling. Make your final act worthwhile. Anyone who intends to commit such a vile act is evil and must be stopped through whatever means necessary. This is one of the few instances in life where there is no compromise and no "grey area." Evil must be vanquished, and anyone who intends to victimize you in such a despicable manner must be made to pay. If you are in disagreement, then I have nothing more to say except that I'm surprised you've read this far. Be safe.

TIPS:

1. It is important to first establish boundaries (physical as well as conceptual) for others to respect, which *are not to be crossed.* The moment someone either enters your "danger zone" or commits a glaring breach of etiquette, your shields should immediately go up. If they continue to push it, after being made aware that they're pissing you off, consider it a preamble to a violent physical attack. If you are isolated, or otherwise feel seriously threatened, immediately launch a pre-emptive strike (Mace Pepperfoam works best for this, as it is easily aimed, produces no residual misting, and the temporary effects do not necessitate emergency medical treatment). You can legitimately claim "self-defense," and if there are no witnesses (or cameras) present, the specific details of what immediately preceded the attack will be known only to yourself and your attacker—simply stated, it will be your word against his.

2. Never willingly place yourself in a position of helplessness—this includes over- imbibing alcohol or sleeping in an unsecured area, as well as accepting rides from strangers or otherwise allowing yourself to be isolated from any possible assistance.

3. Never allow a stranger, or suspicious individual, any opportunity to tamper with your drink (this includes leaving your drink unattended or permitting him to bring you one from the bar). Rohypnol (commonly referred to as "the date rape drug," or "roopies") is available on the black market, and when mixed with alcohol can induce a temporary comatose state in the imbiber. Other additives, like chloral hydrate or barbiturates, are similar, but not nearly as effective. Immediately reject any drink that tastes odd, is gritty, or appears to have oil or powder floating upon the surface.

4. Trust your instincts. "Intuition" can be the result of your subconscious comparing non-verbal cues to past experiences; your olfactory gland registering the nearly imperceptible trace of certain hormones being released; or possibly something even more subtle and incomprehensible, yet real nonetheless. Intuition often proves true—disregard it at your peril.

5. If you believe there is a significant possibility that you are about to be attacked, don't be afraid to scream for help and flee—the worst that can happen is that you'll make a fool of yourself, but you can always exaggerate the facts a bit to justify your "over-reaction" to those who would ridicule you. Temporary embarrassment due to an honest mistake is insignificant and soon forgotten.

6. If bindings are produced (rope, cord, duct tape, zip-ties, wire, or handcuffs), you must not, under any circumstances, allow yourself to become incapacitated! Go completely batshit—kick, scream, throw things, bite, claw, gouge, and use improvised weaponry—but *do not allow yourself to be overpowered!* If he succeeds in binding you, he will then be allowed all the time he needs to enact

his freakish torture and humiliation fantasies before finally discarding your torn and lifeless body in the woods behind a highway rest stop. Do not let this happen.

7. If you must strike, hit hard and accurately, aiming for the eyes, throat, genitals, and knees. If you can seize your attacker's hair, ear, nose, lip, finger, or genitals, yank the part in question with a short and violent motion—if it does not immediately snap off (just like Mr. Potatohead!), twist and tear. Bite holes in any exposed flesh, and use your molars to crush tissue protected by clothing. You need to "step away" for a moment and let *The Demon* take over. With the proper mental preparation, it is a simple matter to compartmentalize your memory of the event in such a way that the details will be difficult to recall. You can train yourself to detach from and forget traumatic events. Don't worry about your "sanity"—if you are a strong individual, you"l be able to deal with what you were forced to do…after all, it's not like you wrongfully injured a *person*.

8. Attacks intended to subdue (commonly employed in the crimes of rape and kidnapping) occur within one's "intimate range." This means that your attacker will come much closer than if he simply intended to beat or threaten you. The best weapon to employ at this range would be a small knife with a comfortable grip, as well as a needle-sharp point (like the *Mini Culloden* from Cold Steel). Such a weapon can be drawn with one hand, sight unseen, and slid into the assailant's gut or kidney with minimal effort. The blade should be driven in to the hilt, then the handle should be repeatedly "pumped" to maximize internal disruption, then twisted hard (prior to retraction) in order to enlarge the wound channel. No strength or skill is required to accomplish this. Such a wound—if delivered correctly—will put an immediate halt to most attacks. Be careful not to lose your grip on the handle! If a quality sheath knife, neck knife, or tactical folder is unavailable to you, a paring

knife or icepick will work nearly as well—a sheath can be fashioned from an old leather belt, or improvised from a piece of
folded cardboard wrapped in duct tape. Never let your assailant
know that you are armed! He should be oblivious to your knife's
existence until the moment it is buried in his torso.

9. If it is definitely going to happen, you are trapped with no means
    of escape, and you feel that you will surely be overpowered if you
    attempt to resist, then you may wish to use deception. Your lies
    and misdirections will depend upon your temperament and the
    circumstances of the situation at hand—and this is something that,
    ideally, you will have thought out well in advance. One example of
    a lie that has been used successfully in the past is to pretend to
    assent to satisfying your attacker's demands, but to state that "it
    would be best" if you were to fellate him due to the fact that "your
    herpes" is currently raging out of control and you "wouldn't want
    him to be angry with you." You could even go so far as to compli-
    ment him or ask him if he "has a girlfriend," but your acting skills
    had better be pretty damn good or he'll know you're trying to trick
    him. Your attacker will be highly suspicious at first, tense, and
    ready to instantly attack, so you'll need to be calm and soothing in
    both tone and mannerisms. Move and speak slowly, and try not to
    appear nervous. If he agrees, you could actually begin to fellate him
    if no other alternative exists, but this is not "giving in" because you
    have a nasty surprise in store for him. He will be on guard and
    ready to attack as you start, but if you pretend to be a submissive
    type who has no intention of fighting back or calling the police, he
    will soon relax—and that's when you chomp down as hard as you
    can, yank your head to the side with as much viciousness as you
    can muster, and immediately spring backwards to avoid the inevi-
    table counter-attack. If your attacker's penis is not severed, it will
    be incredibly mangled, unbearably painful, and incapable of
    inflicting pain upon anyone else in the future—if medical treat-
    ment is not immediately forthcoming, such an injury can easily

result in death through shock, exsanguination, or infection. If emasculation through fellatio is not a viable option, the tongue can be bitten through instead (just be certain to roll clear of the range of *his* teeth, as you could be badly mauled). Again, he will be cautious and need to be taken off guard. This injury will result in massive hemorrhaging, shock, and possibly even death through aspiration of blood.

Be advised, this final tip has not been included frivolously. It amounts to "taking a cut of 1 inch to inflict a cut of 6 inches." True, allowing oneself to be violated may seem inconceivable to many people—especially the true warriors who would prefer to die fighting rather than face "dishonor," but for those persons lacking the capability to inflict serious injury upon a physically superior enemy this might prove a viable alternative. If this technique is performed correctly, the room will be turned into a slaughterhouse, and the horror of what you have done may traumatize you for life, but at least that goblin has *paid* for his crime and will never be able to repeat it again. It is possible that he will still be capable of murdering you, but at least you can die knowing that your attacker will live in impotent misery for the remainder of his pathetic existence. Under no circumstances whatsoever are you to allow yourself to be raped simply in hopes of avoiding further injury, as to play the role of a pacifist in such a scenario will surely result in either death or devastation. If the goblin is misusing his wank he doesn't deserve to keep it. *Don't let him get away with it!*

Unarmed Combat

INTRODUCTION:

Unarmed Combat (often referred to as "Hand-to-Hand" Combat) techniques must be relied upon in the event that one is physically attacked when no weapons, or items that might be employed as improvised weapons, are accessible. Even people who regularly carry a handgun or knife occasionally find themselves in situations where being armed is inconvenient, inappropriate, or prohibited. To those who are familiar with the concept of invisible (improvised) weaponry, almost any common object may be used to defend oneself with varying levels of effectiveness—and as we know, the first rule of Unarmed Combat is to *"arm yourself,"* however, there is the possibility that you could be unexpectedly attacked before having the opportunity to arm yourself, or you could be unlucky enough to find yourself in a setting completely devoid of *anything* that could be picked up and used to inflict injury upon your attacker. Under such dire circumstances, one would be forced to use one's own body as a weapon.

Much has been written about the superiority of certain styles of fighting over others, but self-defense is very different from competing in a martial arts tournament where various rules apply and one is judged by appearances. When you are fighting off a violent attacker who is attempting to maim, rape, or kill you, there will be no restrictions upon your behavior (or that of your adversary) and it would be ludicrous to attempt to implement the difficult spinning kicks that would win you extra points in competition. Techniques should be as simple, efficient, and reliable as possible—which would eliminate: high kicks, throws, sweeps, locks, and "submission holds" for everyone but true experts. Just because you have practiced a move several times with a compliant training partner, there is no guarantee that it will work when confronted with an uncooperative goblin intent upon causing you serious physical harm. Unless you train daily and spar often, most of your "moves" will be forgotten after the first few seconds of a vicious attack on your person—you will be reacting instinctually, without forethought, and if you are unprepared your counterattack may very well prove ineffective.

If you feel threatened by someone, a little switch should automatically click in your head, instantly shifting you into "pre-combat mode." In this state of mind, one becomes hypersensitive to slight changes in the perceived threat's status (proximity, gesticulations, expression, tension, furtive movements, etc.), whilst preparing oneself for the possibility of "fight or flight"—for example, one would probably discreetly scan the area for suitable improvised weaponry. If you *feel* threatened, even though no overt threat has been made, it is highly probable that a *potential* threat exists and should immediately be focused upon. Often, extremely subtle cues indicate danger on a subconscious level, and should not be ignored as "imaginary"—intuition (which primarily consists of making connections with past experiences subconsciously) can be an extremely reliable indicator of an individual's character. It is not "paranoid" to discretely distance yourself from a person whose presence makes you uncomfortable.

If you are blatantly threatened with physical harm (for example, you are roughly shoved backwards, or a weapon is brandished) and feel that the individual(s) in question has the means to seriously injure you, you have the legal right to use a reasonable amount of physical force to protect yourself—*even if you have not yet been harmed* (however, you might be legally required to first attempt a retreat). What constitutes "reasonable force" varies between jurisdictions, but generally is defined as the minimum force required to make the attacker stop his activities—if the court feels that the amount of force used was "excessive" under the circumstances, you would probably be charged with a crime of violence. If a threatening individual has clearly demonstrated that he intends to cause injury to your person, and for whatever reason you are unable to retreat, you are legally permitted to launch a pre-emptive strike. Contrary to popular belief, you are not required to allow your attacker to "hit you first" before fighting back. By his actions of showing clear intent to inflict harm (statements to that effect, closing the distance, and having the means to carry his threats out), he has, in effect, begun his attack even though no blow has yet fallen.

In the event that you are actually grabbed or struck—especially if the attack is unrelenting—and you reasonably believe your life to be in jeopardy, you are legally permitted to use *whatever level of force is required* (including deadly force) to free yourself and flee. As long as you are being immobilized or beaten (provided that you were not the initial instigator), you are allowed to kick, punch, bite, gouge, club, stab, or shoot your attacker into submission, provided that you immediately stop when he no longer poses a threat. Since attackers generally either run in groups or target persons significantly smaller and weaker than themselves, this may not apply.

Generally, any kicks or punches to a threatening adversary of equal or greater size is permissible under the law and would not be looked upon as excessive (provided one's adversary was not laying on the ground or otherwise incapacitated). Biting and eye gouging, however, are considered to be serious attacks capable of maiming, and are only allowed when nothing less than maximum viciousness could enable one to escape. If a court rules that you maimed someone unnecessarily, you could face felony assault charges as well as a lawsuit. It is necessary to exercise restraint.

Unarmed combat techniques usually aren't very effective unless one is highly skilled, as well as physically powerful, and even then success cannot be assured. Empty handed blows inflict only a limited amount of damage. If one wishes to end a conflict quickly or increase one's chances of victory, it is recommended that one use a weapon or some sort of object to attack with. Empty handed blows often prove surprisingly inadequate—even when delivered properly.

THE FUNDAMENTALS:

First, one must possess at least an average degree of physical fitness. If you are a blob or a stickboy, you will be unable to cope with the physical demands of unarmed combat and should instead obtain a carry permit for a handgun and learn how to shoot effectively.

Second, one must be mentally capable of physically striking another person, as well as being struck repeatedly yourself. If you are hesitant to hit someone intent on hurting you, or are fearful of getting injured, getting in trouble, or making an attacker angrier with you, then you need to come to terms with the fact that you are a pathetic weakling dependent upon others for protection. Further progress will be impossible unless this mental block is somehow overcome (visualization and auto-suggestion are the two best methods by which to accomplish this).

Third, you need to forget everything you think you've learned about fighting from watching kung-fu movies and professional wrestling. Hollywood producers have fanciful concepts of the nature of violence, and seldom portray it in a realistic manner.

Fourth, you need to make a commitment to maintain satisfactory physical condition, practice your chosen techniques regularly, practice full-force blows on a heavy bag (or similar target), and occasionally spar full contact with a motivated training partner (if possible).

Finally, one must keep an open mind. Skim through various books on self-defense and martial-arts, absorbing that which is useful and disregarding that which is irrelevant. Many proposed techniques are unworkable for any of a number of reasons (temperament of practitioner, level of skill required, level of conditioning required, little basis in reality, etc.), and certain styles of fighting are best suited for individuals with specific attributes (some favor those with a large bone structure and great strength, whereas others require a high level of endurance combined with blinding speed). Some techniques will be difficult to perform for some individuals, or may have inadequate results, and other moves will be mastered in short order, dependant upon the individual's present capabilities. Generally, one should rely primarily upon movements which feel as natural as possible, if one wishes to minimize his reaction time and maximize his effectiveness. Techniques which feel awkward are best disregarded.

THE BASICS:

Balance is of the utmost importance. If you keep your knees bent and slide your feet, your stance will be far more stable. Formal martial arts stances should be avoided—use whatever natural stance feels most comfortable. Do not over-extend yourself when attacking. Do not cross your legs. Pivot on the balls of your feet.

Avoid incoming blows by sidestepping, bobbing, weaving, and shedding. Block only when necessary, and attempt to *deflect* rather than stop.

Concentrate on your breathing—do not hyperventilate or hold your breath! Remain calm and detached. Most fighters allow themselves to become exhausted within the first two minutes, usually as a result of improper breathing—do not allow yourself to be one of them.

Be aware of what is going on in your vicinity. Do not allow people to enter your blind spots, converge on you in a pincer movement, or back you into a corner. If you are getting a bad feeling about someone, *don't ignore it*! If someone is behaving in a suspicious or threatening manner, don't let them out of your sight. If a stranger attempts to invade your personal space by "getting in your face" or touching you in an inappropriate manner (such as insisting upon shaking hands, putting an arm around you, or placing a hand upon your shoulder), do not hesitate to step back or physically remove their hand—this is not rudeness on your part because, after all, it was *he* who committed the offensive act, not you! If someone who has accosted you suddenly steps closer or slips a hand behind himself where it cannot be seen, call him on it. Case studies have shown that a great many people who had been victimized by criminals knew that something seemed terribly wrong, but they neglected to do or say anything about it because they did not want to be thought of as "rude." Listen up, people: a goblin has no reason to expect courteous treatment from anyone, and he will perceive such as evidence of weakness. If you are perceived as weak, you will be victimized. When you're dealing with miscreants running amok in the street, don't be afraid to act like an asshole. Diplomacy will only result in ridicule.

THE TOOLBOX:

There are a number of body parts which can be used to inflict harm upon another person. These parts include (but are by no means limited to): the hands, the elbows, the feet, the knees, the teeth, and the head. Various fighting styles place emphasis on certain parts over others, or stipulate that the hand be formed in a specific manner when striking. For purposes of brevity, all the various striking surfaces and "hand weapons" will not be addressed, as that would entail a volume of its own; instead, the focus will be on those parts of the body which seem most naturally suited for combat, and which parts of the opponent's body are best targeted by them.

THE HANDS:

One's hands are versatile weapons—they are also the body part most commonly used to strike others with. There are literally dozens of ways to form various "hand weapons" by folding or extending the digits into a variety of shapes. Some of the more natural configurations follow:

1. FIST: The standard closed fist is the most commonly encountered of all hand weapons. The fist typically is clenched into a ball, and the front of the knuckles are used to impact the target. If the head of one's adversary is struck, it is easy to fracture one or more finger-bones. If a solid connection is made with an improperly formed fist, the wrist is often sprained. Only an amateur or a drunk would attempt to smash his unprotected knuckles into solid bone. The

closed fist is best used to deliver uppercut punches to the belly; other targets include the kidneys, spleen, and floating ribs.

2. HAMMERFIST: The hammerfist is similar to the standard fist, except that the edge of the hand is used to contact the target, rather than the knuckles. This hand weapon is instinctively formed by untrained fighters when reacting to a sudden attack, and is universally taught to self-defense students due to the fact that, in a violent confrontation, one's formal training is often forgotten. With this hand weapon, an immense amount of power can be generated with little risk of injury to one's hand as a result. Viable targets for hammerfist blows include: the face (especially the bridge of the nose, the eye socket, and the mandibular joint), the clavicle (collarbone), the kidneys, the spleen, and the back of the elbow (when extended and locked). A reverse hammerfist (which utilizes the thumb side of the hand as the striking surface) can be used to deliver an unexpected rising blow to the groin or belly. This is one of the few hand weapons which can be used to strike the head with minimal risk of injury. It is best used in conjunction with an improvised weapon, such as a fistload (i.e. a roll of coins or an aluminum penlight) or a probe (i.e. a pen, pencil, or chopstick).

3. PALM HEEL: The palm heel is an example of what is commonly referred to as an "open hand strike," which is simply a hand weapon other than a closed fist. This strike is delivered by forcefully thrusting the fleshy base of the palm straight into the target. It is recommended that one's fingers be folded when this strike is delivered, in order to minimize the possibility of accidental breakage. Care must be taken that only the *base* (or "heel") of the palm be used to strike with—if impact is made with the upper portion of the palm, one's wrist can easily become hyperextended. As with the hammerfist, an immense amount of power can be generated with minimal risk of injury. The best targets for this strike include the septum (base of the nose, up under the nostrils) and the jaw

(up under the chin). Other targets include the face, the temple, and the upper portion of the belly just below the sternum (where the xiphoid process is sometimes found).

4. SWAT: The swat (sometimes called a "bear swat" or "iron palm") is essentially the same hand weapon as the palm heel, only it is delivered to the target differently. Instead of a thrust straight into the target's front, the arm is swung horizontally so that contact is made with the target's side. Because of the different angle of attack, connection can be made with the upper portion of the palm without significant risk of injury. The best target for this strike is the face, although anyplace on the head can be struck. The kidneys and spleen are also viable targets. A rising swat can be slammed directly into the groin.

5. EXTENDED KNUCKLE STRIKE: There are many different forms of extended knuckle strike, but the one detailed here extends all four knuckles (and is sometimes referred to as a "leopard punch") and is essentially the same hand weapon as the aforementioned palm heel and swat—although the striking surface has moved to the extended knuckles of the folded fingers. The hand is thrust directly into the target, much like a straight punch. The two best targets for this strike are the throat and the bladder, although the belly could also be attacked. Due to the need for precise accuracy(combined with a significant risk of injury in the event that solid bone is struck) this technique is recommended for advanced students only.

6. CHOP: The chop (often called a "*shuto*"or "knife hand") is another open hand strike which utilizes the edge of the hand to impact the target. Again, it is recommended that one's fingers be folded in order to avoid possible breakage. The small surface area concentrates the force of the blow, but the hand can be injured if solid bone (such as the cranium) is struck. Due to the need for pre-

cise accuracy (combined with the potential risk of fracturing one's hand) this hand weapon is recommended for use by advanced students only. The most favored target for this strike is the throat, which is considered a "killing blow" due to the vulnerability of the windpipe (when chopping at the throat or neck, the entire forearm can be used as a striking surface, if required—such attacks are sometimes referred to as "clothesline" strikes). Other viable targets include: the side of the neck, the back of the neck, the clavicle, the kidneys, and the spleen. Like the hammerfist, the chop can also be reversed.

7.   BACKFIST: Even though the backfist is an inferior technique, it has been included due to the fact that it is favored by many martial artists. The backfist is typically a swinging horizontal blow which uses the first two knuckles on the back of one's closed fist as the striking surface. This can be an incredibly fast, as well as unexpected, technique, but it tends to generate little power and runs a high risk of damage to one's hand. The "temple" region of the skull is usually favored as a target, but as we know, impacting the cranium with one's knuckles is a foolish idea. The nose and the eye socket are both viable targets, however. The backfist is most often used to stun an opponent, making him vulnerable to more powerful blows. Due to the need for pinpoint accuracy (combined with the high risk of potential injury) the backfist strike should only be attempted by an expert martial artist.

THE FINGERTIPS:

While the hands can used to impact an adversary, resulting in contusions and possibly even fractured bones or ruptured organs, the digits can be used to gouge, dig, grasp, and tear, often with horrifying results. Practitioners of fighting systems which implement "maiming" techniques usually strengthen their fingers through exercise and conditioning, and have even been known to actually sharpen their fingernails or use clawlike finger attachments in order to make their strikes deadlier. Growing out the fingernails (usually to between 1/3" and 1/2" in length) is commonly done by some fighters, and a maimer can sometimes be spotted due to the fact that he has cultivated a pair of longish thumbnails, or that the nails of his non-dominant hand (usually the left) are unusually long, yet neatly manicured (long painted fingernails on a male's hands, or a single long pinkie-nail, would tell us something altogether different, however).

Various styles of kung fu (as well as some other martial arts systems) focus on manipulating the fingers into specific shapes to form the hand weapons used for that particular style of fighting. In ancient times, the devastating power of maiming strikes was so feared and respected that kung fu masters kept them as closely guarded secrets, revealed in whole to only a select few students...today, however, any number of martial arts publications will reveal similar techniques to whomever is willing to pay for them. If so many other sources were not readily available, I would have serious reservations about detailing these types of strike. For purposes of brevity, only a few of the possible hand weapons will be detailed here.

1. RIGID HAND STRIKE: The rigid hand strike (also called a "spear" or "shovel" hand) is a blow that can easily cripple the martial artist who attempts it without proper conditioning. Since traditional hand conditioning methods are rarely practiced today, this strike should never be implemented. It has been included due to the fact that it has been featured in many "kung fu movies" and is illustrated in some karate books—some irresponsible instructors even teach it to their students! The rigid hand strike thrusts the fingertips of one's flat hand directly into the target, which can easily hyperextend one's fingers, resulting in possible sprains, dislocations, and fractures. If the hand is slightly curved, the risk of injury is somewhat reduced. In theory, the small surface area of the fingertips results in a highly concentrated blow capable of deep penetration; in practice (with unconditioned hands), greater injury is

usually inflicted upon oneself than upon the recipient. The only targets suitable for attack via this strike are the throat and the belly—both of which would be better attacked using another hand weapon.

2. RIGID EYE GOUGES: There are several popular methods of gouging the eyes of an opponent with one's stiff fingers; as we know, this is a bad idea because a stiff finger is easily broken. The two most common methods involve either making a "V" from the extended fore and middle fingers, or simply fanning all five digits wide apart, then jamming the extended fingers into the opponent's face. Never use rigid fingers to jab at someone's eyes, as you will probably miss the eyes and hurt yourself; even if you *do* contact the eyes, it is unlikely that any serious damage will result. Again, if the fingers are slightly curved, one's risk of injury is somewhat reduced. Due to their inefficiency, these strikes are not recommended for use.

3. FINGERTIP CLUSTER: The "fingertip cluster" hand (sometimes called a "beak hand") is formed by clustering all four fingertips together and resting them atop the thumb for support. It has been included due to the fact that it has been taught to many self-defense students, particularly at "rape prevention" seminars. The fingertips are used to strike repeatedly at the eyes of an attacker, although the throat could be struck as well. With sturdy long nails, as many ladies have, the tip of the beak hand becomes stiff and sharp, which can contribute to an eye injury. Because the fingers are curved as well as clustered together for support, it is unlikely that you will fracture a digit if you miss, however, a fingernail could easily be broken (or bent backwards). Since this is one of the more unusual hand weapons, it will not be instinctively formed, so this strike should be practiced on a regular basis if you intend to add it to your "toolbox." If you are a male, or have fingernails

under an inch in length, other hand weapons would probably prove more effective.

4. EYE DART: The "eye dart" hand is formed by extending the fore and middle fingers, which are pressed together and resting atop the thumb for support. With practice, eye-sized moving targets can be repeatedly struck, and there is a significantly reduced chance of fracturing one's fingers if the cranium is connected with. The eye dart hand can be used to attack either the eye or the throat, but due to the need for precise accuracy (as well as the risk of potential injury) it should be implemented by expert martial artists only.

5. RAKE: The "rake" hand is formed by curling one's separated fingers into a claw. The rake hand is then quickly scraped across an adversary's face in either a downwards or horizontal motion. The dragging nails can inflict abrasions to exposed flesh as well as the surface of the eyes, which could result in pain as well as impaired vision. The rake hand is instinctively formed by those females willing to fight with their nails, and can be used as a stunning blow much like a backfist. Attacks with the rake hand are unlikely to result in serious injury.

6. CLAW: There are about a dozen variants of this hand weapon, most of which are named for kung fu animal styles (eagle, tiger, monkey, etc.). Similar to the rake, the "claw" hand actively digs into the flesh rather than simply being drug across it. With strong hands, not only is it possible to gouge into (and seriously injure) the eyes, but it is possible to actually rip off appendages (i.e. nose, ears, fingers, clumps of hair, male genitals). The appendage in question is firmly grasped, then suddenly snapped away with a specific shearing motion in order to inflict maximum damage. Even incorrect usage of similar techniques can result in tearing lacerations or internal damage. In theory, a master with heavily conditioned hands can rip handfuls of flesh from any part of the body

(although grasping the lip or cheek is not recommended, due to the close proximity of the teeth), pull an opponent's muscles free from their moorings, and even tear out a floating rib or a trachea…however, I have yet to see a credible documented case of this having been done in the past century. Variations of the claw hand (as well as the conditioning techniques required to utilize it effectively) were jealously guarded by the ancient masters, lest they be learned by those who would misuse them, but in our contemporary society wrestlers and streetfighters have been misusing them for years. Maiming techniques are favored by gang members, ex-convicts, and immigrants from certain disadvantaged countries—they are sometimes encountered on the street and in barrooms, so you should familiarize yourself with how the claw hand is used and defended against. This nasty method of ripping people's faces off is something you definitely want to encounter first with a trustworthy sparring partner before being confronted with it for real. Due to the combined factors of pain, horror, and panic, many people suddenly lose their will to fight after sustaining a properly delivered maiming strike.

7. THUMB GOUGE: The thumb is stronger and sturdier than any of the other digits, and if equipped with even a slightly extended nail, it can easily be driven deep into the eye globe, rupturing it and resulting in permanent blindness. If either side of the opponent's head is being grasped, it is possible to rupture both eyes simultaneously, resulting in total loss of vision. Due to the power of this strike, the eye can easily be damaged even through a closed eyelid. This extremely vicious technique is permissible (legally as well as morally) only under actual life-threatening conditions—for which its use is highly recommended. This is one of the rare techniques capable of stopping the vast majority of fights *instantly*.

ELBOWS:

The elbows are one of the body's most powerful weapons. Sturdy and injury resistant, they can be slammed into an opponent from a variety of angles, and are one of the best methods of engaging an attacker who has grabbed you from behind. By twisting one's hips and putting one's full body weight behind an elbow strike, an incredible amount of power can be generated. If desired, the hand of the striking arm can be grasped in order to add more power (the combined force of both arms) to an elbow strike directed at the side or rear. The forearm side and triceps side of the elbow can both be used as striking surfaces as well as the point; although the point of the elbow is bonier and will provide additional penetration, the hinge joint can be damaged if the solid bone of the cranium is connected with. The best targets for elbow strikes are the face and the belly, although nearly any vulnerable area of the head and trunk can be attacked. The elbow strike is probably the only "hand weapon" suitable for crushing ribs, attacking the spine, and safely knocking out teeth. Since there are dozens of variations on the simple elbow strike, it is recommended that you experiment with those techniques which come naturally to you in practice. For further study, information on elbow strikes can be found in nearly every martial arts publication.

THE FEET:

The feet can be the unarmed fighter's most powerful weapons, however, kicks are often misused (even by experienced martial artists), rendering them inefficient or even counter-productive. To immediately clarify things, the two cardinal rules of kicking must be read and absorbed:

1. The feet must be properly shod.

2. Kicks should never be delivered above the waist.

Now, a great many black belts and fans of kung fu movies may disagree with these two simple truths, but the fact remains that kicks with a bare foot (or soft footwear) are far less damaging than kicks delivered with a sturdy boot; and kicks delivered to targets above the waist will be instinctively grasped by even an unskilled fighter, resulting in a substantial risk of capture and immobility.

Proper footwear must be worn in order to get the greatest lethal potential from one's kicks. Soft leather loafers offer no protection to one's vulnerable toes, and most sneakers have shock absorbing rubber soles which will significantly reduce the effect of impact. In order to inflict maximum damage on one's opponent, your optimum choice of footwear should be a boot with a reinforced toe combined with a stacked heel. Such combinations are most often found in work or dress boots. Steel toe caps provide excellent protection for one's toes as well as additional mass to contribute to the force of impact, however, the additional weight can result in a significant reduction in speed. Work boots best suited for kicking include Wellingtons and engineer boots. Dress boots suitable for kicking include square-toed harness boots (often called "snoot boots") and pointy-toed cowboy boots with underslung heels. Whatever style of boot you favor, it should fit tightly enough that it will not fly off your foot if you miss, but should not be so tight as to be uncomfortable. If necessary, a bit of padding could be stuffed within the toe to absorb some of the shock of kicking. Once your feet have been properly shod, any one of the three following kicks may be utilized:

1. TOE KICK: The "toe kick" is the most natural of all possible kicks, and will instinctively be used by any unskilled fighter. It cannot, however, be implemented with a bare or inadequately shod foot, as breakage of one's toes would be a likely result. The foot can be brought directly up into the target area, or it can be cocked back first for additional momentum, and the toe of one's boot is the surface used to make contact. A karate low "snap kick" can also be implemented, using the toe rather than the ball of the

foot as the striking surface. The toe offers excellent penetration versus soft targets (such as the belly), but can successfully be used to inflict damage to any portion of the head, trunk, or limbs of a fallen opponent. Yes, we've all heard that it is "ungentlemanly," or "dirty fighting" to "kick a man when he's down," but if it is likely that he will continue to unlawfully attack you after regaining his footing, what other choice do you have? Do you really think that some goblin who assaults you on the street would extend the same courtesy to you? Rules do not apply unless there is someone there to enforce them fairly and equally, hence, *there are no rules in a streetfight."* Against a standing opponent, the toe kick can be used versus the shin or groin (one's shinbone can be an alternative striking surface for a groin attack, if necessary). Against a doubled-over opponent, a field goal can be kicked into his face. From behind, the coccyx (tailbone) can be struck. Against a prone opponent, the face, head, throat, neck, chest, ribs, spleen, kidneys, belly, and spine can be attacked. Repeated kicks to the head or torso can be fatal, and kicks to the face can easily result is disfigurement (broken teeth and dismoored eyes are common injuries).

2. SIDE KICK: The "side kick" is typically delivered by first "priming" the leg by raising it and twisting the hips, then "firing" it straight towards the target area, contacting it with either the heel or the sole of the boot. With practice, side kicks can be delivered to targets in the front and back as well as either side. In actual combat use, the side kick should be limited to the knee as a target area. If the side of the knee joint is properly struck, the joint can separate, resulting in loss of mobility for the leg in question. The low side kick to the side of the knee joint is another of the rare techniques capable of instantly stopping most fights. If the knee joint is successfully blown out, it will prove extremely painful and corrective surgery (as well as a lengthy period of physical therapy) will be required for it to heal—and full functioning may never be completely restored. If the front of the knee joint is connected with,

the patella (kneecap) can be displaced, resulting in pain and partial loss of mobility, but the front is far inferior to the side as a target. The back of the knee joint can be struck to collapse it, but it is unlikely that serious injury would result.

3. STOMP: The "stomp kick" is typically delivered by first "priming" the leg by raising it, then suddenly slamming it straight down onto a prone opponent. The heel is best used as the striking surface in order to concentrate the blow for greater penetration, although the sole could be utilized instead. A "double stomp kick"can be delivered by leaping into the air and retracting both legs, then suddenly stomping both feet out simultaneously to strike the prone opponent—the double stomp is especially devastating due to one's entire body weight being added to the force of impact, although it is incredibly slow, hence, easily dodged. Stomp kicks are the deadliest foot attack, due to the fact that a prone adversary is trapped against the floor, so all the energy of the blow will be absorbed by his body, resulting in devastating crushing injuries; unfortunately, stomping is extremely common amongst those who engage in group attacks on solitary victims. A stomp to the head can easily crack the skull, and repeated stomps can actually crush it like a melon. Stomps to the torso can easily snap ribs and rupture internal organs, a double stomp would significantly increase the potential for serious injury. A double stomp to the spine can actually snap it, resulting in paralysis below the fractured vertebra—this is the only unarmed attack which has a reasonable expectation of breaking an enemy's back (unless you're slamming around an adversary who's half your size). Stomping on the hands is an excellent tactic, as it renders one's adversary helpless without the risk of inadvertently terminating him. Because a stomping is easy to perform (even by an unskilled attacker) and has potentially lethal results, you never want to find yourself at the feet of your opponent(s). If you are knocked to the floor and cannot immediately regain your footing, you must immediately: kick, sweep, roll, grab,

punch, and bite, but *never stop moving!* If you simply roll up in a fetal position (like many "self-defense" instructors have irresponsibly advised their students to do in such a situation) you will be kicked repeatedly in the back, ribs, and head with no hope of dodging, blocking, or fighting back—basically, you will continue to be kicked until either you are killed or your attacker becomes bored. DO NOT ALLOW YOURSELF TO BE STOMPED!!!

KNEES:

There are a number of ways to use one's knees as weapons. Knees can only be brought into play at extremely close (grappling) range, but they are powerful, injury resistant, and difficult for an opponent to trap. Since it is difficult for most people to use knee strikes effectively, they must be practiced regularly.

The most commonly encountered form of knee attack is the "rising knee strike." In this attack, the leg is suddenly bent and thrust upwards, contacting the target area with the top of the knee, above the patella. The two viable targets for this strike are the groin or the face (of a doubled-over opponent). Another commonly encountered knee attack is the single or double "knee drop", which is similar to a double stomp except that one's body is simply allowed to fall upon one's opponent, knees first. Knee drops are an inferior mode of attack because they have little potential for inflicting serious injury upon one's opponent, and one could suffer a displaced patella in the event that the target is missed; however, this technique is popular among aficionados of televised "professional wrestling." Horizontal knee strikes (sometimes referred to as a "roundhouse knee") can be devastating as well as unexpected, due to the fact that they can attack the spleen, kidneys, or belly from grappling range, but they require a great deal of skill to perform correctly (otherwise little power would be generated or one could be thrown off balance), so they are suitable only for advanced students.

TEETH:

One's teeth are to be considered as the weapons of last resort. Biting can potentially infect the biter as well as the recipient, and such activity is considered repugnant by our society's civilized standards—but it is potentially the most damaging of any unarmed attack. If an unpracticed fighter attempts a "maiming" open hand strike for the first time against a real opponent, there is a good possibility that the results will be unsatisfactory; but if that same fighter were instead to latch onto his opponent with his teeth, he would be assured of drawing blood (at the very least). Teeth can cause major damage.

Believe it or not, there are a number of ways to bite one's enemy. If, for example, an attacker were to cover your mouth with his hand, you could: sink your teeth into his palm, chomp down on the side of his hand, or even crack off a finger. The front teeth (incisors and canines) are best suited for ripping away hunks of flesh, while the back teeth (molars) are best suited for cracking and pulverizing small bones (like the phalanges and metacarpals). Depending on how a bite is delivered (location, pressure, motion, and teeth utilized), it may bleed profusely or not at all (crushing bites often result in internal bleeding only). Any area of exposed (or even clothed) flesh which can be brought into contact with the mouth can be bitten into, so biting can be considered to be one of the most versatile of attacks.

If an enemy can be bitten upon the face, portions of the nose and ear can easily be severed, or the cheek can be ripped into and torn open. The neck could also be chomped upon, crushing muscles, inducing bleeding, and possibly even exposing the trachea. The limbs and torso can also be bitten into, with various results (the exposed blood vessels inside the wrist and elbow are highly vulnerable to this form of attack). While biting can cause horrific disfigurement, it is unlikely to result in immediate fatality; although death could result after the altercation from blood loss, or much later from infection (as human bites often turn septic). Contrary to popular belief, it is highly unlikely that one could successfully bite another man's throat out (either the windpipe or the major blood vessels)—it would be extremely difficult to do so unless one had previously practiced extensively on a specially constructed target of some sort.

When one's teeth are sunk into one's enemy, they should be clenched as tightly as possible before ripping the head to the side in a sudden shearing motion. If the molars are being utilized to crush tissue or bone, one's jaw could be ground. After one chunk of flesh has been torn free, it should immediately be spat away so you can latch on again and again. For a chilling example of how one's teeth can effectively be used as a weapon, view the old horror movie *Dawn of the Dead*. Now that you can see how damaging a bite can be, you'll be far more likely to avoid allowing any part of yourself to come within close proximity of the teeth of your adversary—who might show no reluctance whatsoever at taking a big meaty chunk out of *you*.

THE HEAD:

There are several ways to use one's head as a weapon, but most of them put one at significant risk of injury. The safest way to headbutt someone is to repeatedly slam the back of your head into the face of someone who has grabbed you from behind—this will mash his nose flat with little chance of hurting yourself in the process. In order to headbutt someone in front of you, the best way is to suddenly lurch forward, slamming your upper forehead or top of the skull directly into his face with the intent of crushing the nose. Some idiots think it is macho to smash their forehead against the bony forehead of another, or even to actually charge someone (like a bull) from across the room with the apparent intent of ramming the top of their head into the belly of their adversary—if you are stupid enough to try either of these slick moves, you *deserve* to wind up in the emergency room. The chief advantage of a properly executed headbutt is the element of surprise—when performed correctly, it is nearly impossible to dodge.

HOW TO FIGHT:

Each individual who has fought, or considered fighting, has a fighting style specific to their abilities and needs; however, a few basic rules should always be adhered to:

1. Before the situation escalates into an actual fight, decide what options you want to pursue. Can the situation be defused by saying a few conciliatory words and moving away? Can someone else (like a friend, bouncer, or policeman) immediately intervene on your behalf? Will a swat to the face be sufficient to eliminate the threat, or is it necessary to blow out his knee? Are you in genuine fear for your life, or is this just a petty squabble? These things need to be considered before you react violently to provocation.

2. Rather than lashing out impulsively and blindly, one should target an adversary's vulnerable areas, attacking them with precision.

3. If any form of improvised weapon becomes available, do not hesitate to arm yourself with it.

4. Attack first.

5. Attack viciously.

6. Never give up.

7. Do not stop attacking until the threat has been eliminated (due to its incapacitation or retreat).

8. If a deadly weapon is drawn, or if multiple adversaries are involved, you could not reasonably be accused of cowardice for fleeing—unless it was imperative that you stayed and protected someone who was unable to flee. Sometimes running away is the best available option.

HELPFUL TIPS:

1. Make full use of improvised (particularly bludgeons and missles) and environmental (i.e.: walls, floors, doors, tables, stairs, pits, curbs, traffic, and fire hydrants) weaponry.

2. If a solid connection is made with your adversary's nose, his eyes will flood with tears, impairing his vision.

3. A quick flick of the fingers towards the eyes is often enough of a distraction to enable you to either land a telling blow or flee the area.

4. Once you get a firm grasp on the hair or ears, the adversary's head can be more easily led into either a wall or a rising knee strike.

5. An open hand strike utilizing the notch between the thumb and forefinger as a striking surface can be jammed into an opponent's throat to stun, stagger, or kill, depending upon the level of force used.

6. If grasped, the little finger of the offending hand can easily be wrenched backward and snapped off.

7. If the fore and middle fingers of an opponent's hand can be grasped with one hand, and the ring and little fingers of the same hand can be grasped with the other, it is possible to actually rip his hand in half by peeling the two sides in opposite directions. Be advised—this is a particularly messy technique.

8. If you succeed in hooking two fingertips into your opponent's nostrils, it is possible to peel his nose off his face by suddenly jerking it upwards, shearing the moorings. If you pull someone's nose off, you'll be able to see his tonsils.

9. The deadliest way to choke an opponent facing you is to grasp the neck so the full pressure of the thumbs can be used to crush the windpipe. Simply squeezing the throat or applying pressure to the blood vessels often proves ineffective as the subject panics and begins fighting harder. Remember, if both hands are used to attack the throat, you will be unable to block incoming blows.

10. If the spleen (found on the left side of the torso under the ribs—consult an anatomy chart for the precise location) is ruptured, your opponent can bleed out internally; if the full bladder (as bladders tend to be in drinking establishments) is struck, it can rupture and make your body go into toxic shock; if the kidney is struck, it can hemorrhage. Strikes to these areas formed the legend of the "delayed death touch."

11. The elbow can easily be hyper-extended by straightening the arm into a locked position and either swatting the back of the elbow joint, or laying it across one's knee (or shoulder) and yanking downwards. By bending the arm backwards and twisting sharply, the shoulder can be dislocated. If either the lower or upper arm has popped out of its socket, the joint is held together by nothing more than soft tissue which can be twisted and torn. Due to these facts, it is possible for a highly motivated attacker to actually rip his opponent's arm off.

12. Grinding one's knuckles or fingertips: up under the jaw, into the hollow behind the ear, inside the upper arm, inside the wrist, or inside the armpit can be excruciatingly painful if the proper points are manipulated correctly. Attacking pressure points takes months of practice to have any chance at success, so these moves are recommended for advanced students only, with the understanding that they will only work about half the time.

CONCLUSION:

You now possess the basic foundation for a highly effective method of unarmed combat. This once secret knowledge can enable *anyone* to better defend themselves. Further study as well as intensive practice (utilizing heavy bags as well as sparring partners) is required, however, in order to gain the experience and confidence you'll need to prevail. Remember, your attitude is the primary factor which will determine whether you'll be the victim or the victor. Big muscles, martial arts training, and even a weapon will all be useless if you lack the heart to win. If you are a whimpering coward, with no vestiges of dignity in the face of violent opposition, your enemy shall soon put you in your rightful place. Stand up for yourself, because you can't always count on others to protect you. If you refuse to stand up for yourself, you are actually giving others *permission* to victimize you! *"It is better to die on one's feet than live on one's knees."* Don't be a weakling!

Invisible Weapons

What is an invisible weapon? It is a common everyday item, either carried on one's person or found in one's immediate vicinity, which can quickly be brought into use as an improvised weapon if required. Because literally *anything* can be used to injure, stun, or disorient another individual, it is nearly impossible to regulate such items. However, if a dangerous implement is discovered on your person (or in your car), you may be asked to explain its purpose and necessity—if your explanation is unsatisfactory, you may face a misdemeanor weapon possession charge. A similar charge might be added to a battery offense if any household object, however innocuous, was used to strike the other person. Yes, it is possible to face a weapons charge for striking your attacker with a hairbrush, coffee cup, or children's toy. In many jurisdictions, *any* object that is used as a weapon becomes a weapon, as so recognized by the letter of the law.

This section will deliberately be kept brief. There are dozens of books available which describe how hundreds of household objects are best employed to inflict injury upon another person. A few of these books are entirely devoted to the subject of improvised weaponry. Some of these books are very good, whereas others contain much misinformation and unproven theory. For example, two respected authors of self- defense literature state, in their separate books, that you can easily inflict a lethal injury by stabbing someone with a plastic drinking straw (in theory, if one's thumb is covering the end, the trapped air will make it rigid enough to penetrate the abdominal wall or throat), and that you can use the discarded lid from a soup can as an effective substitute for a throwing star! In theory, both of these statements are correct, but would you risk using such flimsy weapons when virtually anything else would prove far more effective? In practice, effective blows with a drinking straw or soup can lid can be delivered about 10% of the time (using a watermelon as the target medium)—you would have much better odds with a teaspoon or ashtray. Several publications suggest that one use a lit cigarette (or any open flame) to turn a can of hairspray (or spraypaint, WD-40, or similar flammable aerosol) into an "effective flamethrower"…please do not attempt such folly under any circumstances whatsoever! Such a "flamethrower" only has an effective range of about two feet, is unlikely to inflict even minor injuries to an assailant (the spray is consumed instantly), and will explode in your hand if the flame enters the can's nozzle (engulfing you in a fireball and peppering you with shrapnel). Other examples include references to matchbooks and wire clotheshangers as "lethal weapons." Improvised weapons manuals, like most popular martial arts publications, tend to grossly exaggerate the effectiveness of their methods—thus, a modicum of common sense is required. The finest book available the subject of improvised weaponry is <u>Black Medicine Vol. 2 (Weapons at Hand)</u> by Dr. Mashiro and published by Paladin Press. It is required reading for any serious student interested in the subject matter.

As I have said before, it is better to strike with a readily available object that to use one's empty hand. Not only will a rigid or pointed object tend to do more damage, but the chance of injury to your hand will be greatly reduced. As I have said above, numerous volumes have been devoted to the subject of improvised weapons, and many can be ordered from your local bookstore, so I am not going to waste time and space by transcribing reams of easily procured material. Instead of listing hundreds of tools, utensils, and objects which can be found in any home, office, or dumpster; I will instead focus on objects commonly found on (or near) one's person. Using the elements of surprise and precision targeting, most can be relied upon to startle or stun an adversary, thus allowing ample opportunity for escape.

HELMET: Protective headgear worn for motorcycling, bicycling, skating, or other sports will add a new dimension to the several versions of headbutt. As an added bonus, helmets can be grasped by the chinstrap and swung like a short flail—motorcycle helmets in particular are incredibly effective in this capacity. A swung helmet is best used against the head, face, elbows, hands, and knees.

HATPIN: The ladies' hatpin is often referred to in self-defense literature, even though they are seldom seen nowadays. A long shafted hatpin or hairpin can be worn as intended or pinned to a jacket as a brooch. They are often somewhat flimsy, but are good for a single deep thrust into soft tissue. The best targets are the eye, throat, neck, solar plexus, and kidney. Even if a flawless thrust is delivered deep into a vital area, it is unlikely that your attacker will be immediately killed; indeed, he may not realize he is seriously injured until he eventually weakens from internal bleeding, as the initial shock will be minimal and puncture wounds seldom bleed profusely unless a major artery has been pierced. It is possible to jab a long pin upwards beneath the sternum to pierce the heart. A hatpin will not penetrate the skull.

EYEGLASSES: I have included spectacles because they have been mentioned in numerous publications. Some "experts" seem to think that you can grasp your glasses in your hand to add power to a hammerfist strike, or use the temples to gouge your attacker's eyes—this is asinine. Eyeglasses are a flimsy and inefficient weapon, and are guaranteed to be broken beyond repair if you attempt to use them in this manner. Provided you have shatterproof plastic lenses, it is best to leave your glasses in place to provide limited protection for your vulnerable orbs.

KEYS: Nearly every self-defense manual I've seen advises people to "make a fist with your keys protruding from between your fingers, creating a set of vicious claws." Never attempt this. Not only is it difficult to get the keys into position under stress, but it is uncomfortable, and the keys are far more likely to twist and cut into the tendons and nerves of your digits rather than seriously injure your opponent. Keys are best implemented as a flail when swung at the end of a neckcord, lanyard, chain, or tasseled fob. Such a flail is best used against the face, but a heavy ring of keys will do injury wherever it hits. The penlights commonly seen attached to keyrings are usually too small to utilize as an impact weapon, but they do provide a grip for your improvised flail. Plastic and aluminum fistloads (some designed with dual rods that extend between the fingers) are designed to serve as keyrings, but are considered weapons in a few misguided localities. Small pepperspray canisters also may be attached to one's keyring. Miniature pushdaggers with attached keyrings are also sold, but tend to be slow into action and are prohibited in many jurisdictions. Keys can be thrown into an attacker's face, but that would be a foolish thing to do under most circumstances, when a handful of dirt or gravel would have a similar effect.

PEN: A sturdy metal pen can be firmly grasped and used to stab shallow holes into an opponent reasonably well. The Parker "Jotter," fashioned from stainless steel and priced at about $7, works remarkably well in this capacity, though more expensive filigreed pens provide a surer grip. Pens, and similar implements, used as weapons are usually held one of three ways: extending from the bottom of the fist, extending from the top of the fist, or braced against the palm and extending between the fingers of the fist. Contrary to what some "experts" claim, it is difficult to pierce the skull with a pen unless you are a powerlifter who is holding your target's head motionless against the floor before striking with all your strength—an unlikely turn of events. Disposable plastic ballpoints can be used, but are far less effective due to their tendency to bend or shatter upon impact. Pens are best used against the eye and throat, but other viable targets include the temple, solar plexus, kidney, and up under the chin. Pencils and chopsticks also work well in this capacity. There are many styles of "pen" with concealed blades or spikes inside, but these are generally cheaply made and slow into action, as well as being prohibited in some jurisdictions. There are several styles of "pen gun," usually firing a single .22 LR cartridge, but these are more suited for assassinations as they tend to be too awkward to ready instantly or too unsafe for continuous carry. Pens that discharge pepperspray usually have an extremely short range, but a few quality models exist. Pen-style flare projectors are far too unsafe to carry loaded, and how would you explain one's presence to the authorities?

COMB: When handled by a skilled martial artist, a steel comb can be used to deliver terrible ripping gashes, crack bones, or even trap a blade. A "rat-tail" comb (even a plastic one, when sharpened) can be used to stab and gouge. Steel hair picks can be used to puncture and tear. Several companies offer combs and brushes that pull apart to reveal a synthetic blade affixed to the handle. A wooden hairbrush makes an effective bludgeon.

PENLIGHT: Small aluminum penlights, particularly the "2-AA" size, serve as effective yawaras (weighted fistloads). When grasped firmly, a forceful hammerfist blow to the skull can result in a fracture. The most effective target would be the temple. Several companies offer a weighted replacement buttcap for the Mini Mag-Lite that not only augments its potential as a yawara, but actually allows one to club with it as well (to a limited capacity, of course).

WRISTWATCH: One's wristwatch can be slipped over the knuckles, resulting in a more damaging impact surface; however, your knuckles will not be protected from injury unless you have a thick leather band with the watch mounted on top. Wide leather watchbands offer limited protection against knife cuts and blunt trauma to the wrist.

BELT: Belts can be used to block, bind, and choke, as can a shirt or scarf. They can also be used as an effective flail. A leather belt with heavy buckle can be wrapped once or twice around one's hand and used to strike with. A substantial buckle constructed of silver, brass, or pewter can be swung with the speed of a *nunchaku*, and will easily fracture a skull. Lighter buckles can be counted on to inflict stinging welts and small lacerations. A concho belt (worn outside the loops) can inflict injury along its entire length. A belt can be rolled repeatedly around the knuckles to punch with and swing like a blackjack in close quarters, or it can be extended to strike at targets over a yard away—it is often swung in variations of a "figure-8" pattern, or whipped horizontally, vertically, or diagonally. When swinging a belt with force, you will occasionally strike yourself—this is unavoidable (although the buckle's velocity is considerably reduced after passing the apex of its swing). With practice, you will learn to take a reduced power blow to the back and thigh, as well as allow the belt to wrap around your arm, rather than having the buckle unexpectedly impact the back of your head. After much practice, you can trap weapons, throw opponents, and snag a wrist or ankle at a distance. Every martial artist and self-defense student should practice drawing and swinging the belt, as it is clearly among the finest of improvised weapons.

WALLET: If being relieved of one's possessions, one's wallet can be tossed in a distracting manner (in a high arc, or even directly into the face) as a precursor to a blade or empty-handed attack. Or, it can be tossed to the ground, where an attack can be launched as he stoops to pick it up. If you pretend to be frightened and compliant, it is unlikely that such an attack would be expected.

CREDIT CARD: The credit card has been included because it too has been touted as "highly effective" by several self-defense authors. If you have a few seconds to get ready, and no other weapons are available (unlikely), a credit card or similar piece of plastic can be snapped in two, and grasped in either hand. Many types of plastic card have sharp edges when snapped, while others do not, so there is no guarantee this will work. Some credit cards already have an edge which can be honed sharp with emery paper. If you choose to prepare a credit card in advance for everyday carry, both corners of one end can be broken off to form a point before sharpening. Targets include the forehead, eyes, throat, and inner forearms. A skilled martial artist can grasp even an unaltered card in his hand, using a single corner to deliver concentrated force to vulnerable nerve cavities and exposed blood vessels. However, if the wielder is not an expert at unarmed combat and the assailant is not able to be taken by surprise with the first blow, a credit card is little better than useless.

SINKER: A lead fishing sinker, weighing 2 or 3 ounces, can be affixed inside one's cap with a safety pin or dropped inside one's pocket attached to a length of fishing line. Swung properly, this innocuous looking item can easily crack a skull.

WASHERS: A few large steel washers (1" inner diameter, and approx. 1/5 pound each) can be slipped in one's pockets for discreet carry. With practice, they can be thrown (overhand, backhand, or underhand) with a great deal of force as well as surprising accuracy. Bouncing a few of these off an assailant from twenty feet away can inflict painful bruises and lacerations, possibly making him reconsider pursuit.

LOLLY: One of the fancy "gourmet" lollipops, with the round head and a wooden stick, can be grasped so the stick protrudes from either the base of the fist or between the knuckles, allowing one to puncture an eye, or poke deep into the throat (or the soft flesh under the jaw).

COINS: A plastic wrapped roll of nickels makes an excellent fistload, and a handful of pennies can be tossed into an assailant's face. With practice, silver dollars can be stuck in a wall from thirty feet away with great accuracy. The ancient Chinese sometimes carried sharpened coins that functioned like throwing stars—a similar weapon can be fabricated by sharpening the edge of large brass washers, but much better weapons can be procured with far less effort. A drawstring pouch used as a change purse makes an excellent (as well as legal) improvised blackjack.

FOOTWEAR: Sturdy footwear is necessary to deliver effective kicks. The French Canadian lumberjacks who perfected Savate knew that heavy workboots were far more damaging than unshod feet. Kicks delivered with sneakers, loafers, and sandals are often even less effective than a conditioned unshod foot due to the soft toes and rubber soles. A boot with a substantial toe and heel works best. Pointed toe cowboy boots can do almost as much damage as steel-toed workboots. Protective steel and plastic toecaps are available in sneakers and dress shoes as well as boots. Steel toes add power to your kicks, but reduce speed. A stacked heel, such as is found on most cowboy boots and some engineer boots, can deliver crushing blows to fallen opponents. Dress shoes, such as wing-tips and oxfords, can either be grasped by the toes or slipped onto the hands and used to pummel one's opponent. A woman's stiletto heels are best removed and grasped in the hands to serve as blunt picks with which to attack the head, torso, and arms.

SOCK: A sock, or nylon stocking, becomes a deadly flail when a stone, perfume bottle, or handful of sand is dropped inside and knotted off—of course, this requires a few moments of advance preparation. If you want a preassembled weapon, a D-cell battery makes a fine weight. If preassembled, it should not be knotted if there is any possibility of being stopped and frisked by the local constabulary, so as to give you opportunity to allow the weight to drop out prior to examination. Such a weapon is considered a blackjack or sandclub, which are prohibited weapons.

ATTACHE CASE: An attache case, laptop computer, or lunchbox can be swung as a bludgeon. Upwards swings to the knee, groin, or chin are often unexpected. The attache case can also serve as a shield against knife attacks, but the best defense is a good offense. Clipboards can also be used as shields, but are better used to inflict crushing lacerations with the narrow edges. With practice, both the attache case and clipboard can be thrown with great force and accuracy.

DOG LEASH: Thin chain leashes make nasty whips that will cause any attacker to pause and weigh his options. Leather and nylon leashes can be swung to impact with the clasp, or they can be used to block, bind, or choke. Leashes can be used in a similar manner as belts, but with more flexibility. If a training collar—especially a prong (pinch) collar—is attached to the end, it will serve as a wicked flail. Of course, if your dog is aggressively protective of you, that is an additional benefit.

CANE: There are schools devoted exclusively to cane fighting, and there are literally dozens of ways to use a crookneck cane as a weapon. In addition to being swung like a rod or jabbed like a spear, it can trip, trap, and deliver unexpected hooking attacks. Walking sticks also make good weapons, especially when fitted with a ferrule and heavy metal grip. Walking sticks made of rattan, blackthorne, and exotic hardwoods are popular, as well as effective. Steel and leaded canes can deliver devastating blows, but are prohibited in some jurisdictions. Sword canes and cane guns are illegal almost everywhere. If you are not lame, and are carrying a cane in an urban environment, you may be harassed by police who could conceivably charge you with weapon possession if you can't convince them you have an injured knee or bad back. A stout walking stick will cause injury anywhere it hits, but is best used versus the arms and knees. Strikes to the head should not be attempted until your opponent is sufficiently worn down. Many experts recommend that a cane or stick should be grasped like a quarterstaff and used primarily to jab with, rather than swung like a bat, which could make it easier for an attacker to slip through your defenses or wrest your stick away.

UMBRELLA: Contrary to popular belief, the umbrella is a poor weapon. When closed, it can be used to jab with, but will often bend or break almost immediately. When open, it is best used as a shield with which to momentarily blind your opponent before a kick to the knee is delivered.

NEWSPAPER: A newspaper or magazine, tightly rolled, can be used to jab deep into the throat or solar plexus, and it is possible to inflict serious injury or death if used correctly. The rolled newspaper or magazine, however, is ineffective to swat with unless the nose is struck directly—such a flimsy weapon relies heavily upon the element of surprise. A newspaper, tightly rolled and folded over at either end, can be grasped in the fist so as to cover the knuckles, protecting them from injury as you strike full force blows to the head and body; with the knuckles protected in such a manner, it is possible to repeatedly punch a brick wall without shattering your hand. Even a single sheet of paper can become a weapon after a few moments of folding—and you don't even need to know origami! The sheet is simply repeatedly folded accordion style, then folded over once and grasped in the fist. The densely packed paper becomes an effective yawara with which to enhance the impact of hammerfist blows.

ASHTRAY: The contents of an ashtray can be directed into an assailant's face to impair vision. The ashtray itself can be used as a bludgeon or projectile. A lit cigarette can be ground into exposed flesh to startle an attacker into releasing his grip on you, but is unlikely to repel anyone but a wussy.

BEVERAGE: Steaming hot coffee can be splashed in an attacker's face to immediately stop all but the most determined of assaults, but it will scald and distract even if the face is missed. The mug can be grasped by the base and used to hammer with. A coffee mug can easily crack a skull. A glass bottle can be thrown with great accuracy, after practice, and can shatter upon contact. You should practice throwing bottles with varying amounts of fluid. A bottle can also be used as a bludgeon which can shatter into an edged weapon—for numerous reasons, the bottle should never be shattered deliberately (it could disintegrate, cutting your hand or sending a glass fragment into your eye). Any beverage can be splashed into the face, and any glass or rigid plastic receptacle can be used to strike with—from shot glasses to pitchers.

Beverages with a high alcohol content can also be set ablaze. Unopened cans can be thrown, used to hammer with, or placed within a sack, towel, or T-shirt to serve as an improvised flail. Empty cans can be torn in half and used to cut with.

FOOD, FLATWARE, AND UTENSILS: Yes, it is possible for your vittles to become weaponry, but in most cases they will simply serve as a diversion when thrown into the face of an attacker. Hot soup can scald, and a plate of hot food fresh from the oven will be doubly unpleasant to have tossed in one's face. A bone can be used to hammer or tear with, depending upon its configuration. A pepper (or even salt or parmesan cheese) shaker can have its lid removed before tossing its contents in an attacker's face with a sweep of the arm—after which, the empty container can be thrown or used to hammer with. Plates can be tossed like frisbees—or (if they are glass) they can be broken and used to cut with. Cooking pots and skillets can be used as bludgeons. Serving forks, skewers, and knives all can be used to stab with. One's fork and spoon can cause serious injury, possibly death, if used forcefully(provided they are silver or steel—aluminum will deform upon impact, lessening the desired results, and plastic utensils should not even be considered—even when broken, they seldom are jagged enough to scratch with). Chopsticks can be held several different ways and used to jab deep into soft tissue. Glass ketchup bottles, jars of condiments, and metal napkin dispensers all are excellent missile weapons. Cloth napkins and tablecloths can become flails upon insertion of a properly sized heavy object (like a rock, or condiment jar).

CHAIR: Chairs are generally lousy weapons. If thrown or swung, they are easily dodged. If you are fit, a folded metal chair can be grasped by the legs and swung horizontally, but you will be vulnerable if you miss and overextend yourself, spinning yourself around. If your attacker has a knife, a stool or lightweight wooden chair can be grasped by the seat (or back) and the legs can be used to jab with while providing a shield that can keep him at bay (as well as possibly trap his arm).

ENVIRONMENTAL WEAPONS: These are aspects of your immediate surroundings which can be used to injure or kill an opponent when no other weapon is available or feasible. A few significant examples would include: pushing your assailant into a busy street, off a roof, out a window, or down a flight of stairs; slamming him into a wall, heavy appliance, or outside corner of a building; slamming his head against the floor, sidewalk, or curb; slamming his head or arm in a door; or striking him over the head with a mirror, wall clock, or toilet tank lid. Falling against (or being thrown against) a solid immovable object will do far more damage than falling in the soft grass or getting struck with a fleshy hand. Weapons are all around you...open your eyes and contemplate this simple, yet profound, truth.

Beltfighting

The belt is among the finest of all improvised weapons. It is legal, always readily available, and devastatingly effective. It can be used at ranges from four feet to six inches, it is incredibly quick, and will leave welts or lacerations wherever it hits. Whipped in a blur and swung in a tight figure-8, the belt becomes an intimidating weapon. In skilled hands, it can easily defeat a knife, a club, or multiple unarmed opponents. It is a popular weapon, having been used in streetfights and barroom brawls for decades. It is often pulled in situations where a weapon is required, but drawing a knife or gun might be considered too extreme—while it is possible to kill with a belt, it is difficult to do so accidentally. To observe a beautiful display of beltfighting, you can rent <u>Fist of Legend</u> starring Jet Li (he uses the belt in many of his films).

BELT SELECTION:

There are two basic styles of belt—light and heavy. You will need to decide which style to favor, but you should strive for proficiency with both. The belts you choose should be comfortable, flexible, durable, stylish, and able to clear your belt loops without binding or snagging.

Examples of light belt would include thin leather dress belts and web belts with roller buckles. The belt should be durable as well as flexible. The buckle should be bare metal rather than encased in leather or other material. Square buckles with sharp corners should be favored over smooth rounded buckles. The thicker and heavier the buckle is, the more effective your strikes will be. Light belts are very quick; are effective for snapping at the face and hands; and are good for wraps, traps, and locks.

Heavy belts are typically wide leather belts, such as garrison or western style, fitted with a substantial buckle fashioned from brass, silver, or pewter. Optimally, the buckle should weigh about a pound. Large, square brass buckles, such as are found on garrison belts, may be sharpened along the edges or just at the corners (using a file and sandpaper, before honing with a whetstone). Whatever buckle you choose should be securely fixed to the belt. If it is simply held in place by a pair of snaps, stitching or super glue may be in order to prevent it from unexpectedly flying away. The heavy belt may not be as quick or as flexible as the light belt, and it is ill suited for fancy techniques, but the oversized buckle can be counted upon to deliver debilitating crushing blows. Used correctly, it can break bones with every strike.

Some people favor concho belts, which can do damage along their entire length. The ones that are segmented have the best flexibility. Concho belts, however, must be worn outside the belt loops to prevent snagging.

I have seen belts fashioned from motorcycle drive chains. These are often chrome plated and fitted with a special buckle. While these belts are indeed effective bludgeons, they are uncomfortable, inflexible, highly visible, and far too heavy for daily wear…besides, they make you look like a cartoon character.

Every month, your belts should be examined for wear. Belts that are exhibiting cracking or dry rot should be replaced.

DRAWING:

First, be aware that pouches, holsters, and clips (for knives or pagers) that depend on your belt for support may prevent your belt from being pulled free. Clips will invariably snag, but pouches and sheaths may simply drop to the ground. If you intend to use your belt as a weapon, and would like to be able to draw it quickly, do not attach anything to it.

You should be able to unbuckle and pull free your belt quickly with one hand. This will take hours of practice to perfect, so you can do so in a single fluid motion. Once freed, you will be grasping the buckle end. While the leather end can be used to slap with, and can even do significant damage if fitted with a decorative metal tip, it is advised to use the buckle as your primary striking surface. It is important to practice readying your belt less than a second after it has been drawn. Only after having gained proficiency at instantly drawing and readying your belt can it be relied upon to protect you.

RANGE:

The belt can be used at a variety of ranges, depending upon how many times it is wrapped around one's hand. Wrapped not at all, but simply grasped in the hand, a size 36 belt gives you an effective range of approximately one yard beyond your outstretched arm. Wrapped once, the range will be reduced to about 30", depending upon factors such as hand width and tightness of wrap. Wrapped twice, range will be reduced to about 24", which is optimal for most defensive applications, giving you a good balance between range and control. Wrapped five or six times, you will have a leather boxing glove with a short blackjack attached.

Wrapping the belt around your hand will both prevent droppage and protect the knuckles against cuts or impact; however, such wrapping effectively attaches the belt to your hand, and you could be yanked off balance if the belt is grabbed by your opponent—even if you release your grasp. I recommend wrapping your hand only twice, before swinging the belt so viciously that few adversaries would have the courage to attempt to snatch it.

BASIC MOVEMENTS:

The Japanese have an entire fighting style devoted solely to using the belt as a weapon, known as *obijutsu*, and the belt is one of the traditional weapons of the eclectic Korean style known as *hapkido*. It takes at least five years for a skilled martial artist to achieve true mastery. I could devote an entire volume to all the various aspects of beltfighting, but that would go way beyond the scope of this project. Marines, bikers, cowboys, and other violent individuals familiar with streetfighting seldom rely on fancy tricks that take years of practice to perform properly—they favor simple techniques that show immediate results with a minimum of preparation. Since self-defense techniques have much more in common with streetfighting than classical martial arts, we shall focus primarily upon the quick and nasty moves. If you have never used a flexible weapon before and are nervous about injuring yourself with the buckle, you can either remove the buckle or use a length of rope until you become more comfortable (wussy). The belt is far safer to use than the *nunchaku, manrikikusari,* or *kusari-fundo.*

1. THE FIGURE-8: This is the first movement you should learn. After wrapping your hand once or twice, slowly swing the buckle in a wide horizontal figure eight in front of your body. After you feel comfortable doing this, you can swing the buckle in the same pattern on either side of your body as well. Next, you can practice tightening and loosening the pattern. After that, you can practice vertical figure-8s and alternate between swinging the belt far from and close to your body. Finally, you can increase your speed. The figure-8 is the most efficient pattern for introductory beltfighting, being easily learned and intimidating to face. It forms a whirling shield of pain from which dozens of attacks can be initiated without warning.

    Some self-defense "experts" advocate whipping one's belt in a circular motion over one's head to deter assailants, but that is silly as well as ineffective.

2. FLAGELLATION: When practicing or fighting with flexible weapons, you will occasionally hit yourself—this is an eventuality, and is to be expected. In practice, you will learn to redirect a missed swing or rebounding buckle so that it misses you, wraps

harmlessly around your arm, or strikes a low-injury area at reduced speed.

You should practice swinging your belt back and forth horizontally, allowing it to wrap around your body and strike your back. By wrapping and unwrapping your hand, you can see how the buckle will impact you at various ranges, so you have a better idea of what to expect. Remember, the buckle's velocity will be considerably reduced after passing the apex of its swing. With practice, you can learn to redirect missed swings, sidestep them, or allow the belt to wrap harmlessly around your forearm without striking you. In the event that you cannot avoid being struck, chances are the impact will not result in injury if you've been training properly.

3. RANGE ADJUSTMENT: While practicing attacks from the figure-8 pattern versus your imaginary opponent, you should also practice extending and shortening your range by wrapping and unwrapping your hand "on the fly." This is done one- handed, and results in a nearly instant adjustment. Maximum range is used for snagging wrists and ankles, snapping into the face, or keeping a knife wielder at a safe distance. A single wrap gives you a better grip, and is good for keeping multiple opponents at bay. A double wrap gives you the best grip, and is good for serious fighting at close range. Additional wraps make your grip increasingly uncomfortable as well as drastically reducing your range, but this might be necessary for certain applications, such as grappling or sapping.

4. THE SLAP: This technique has a low potential for inflicting serious injury, and is ideal for times when only moderate use of force is required. The buckle end is grasped in the hand, and either the extended or doubled leather strap is used to strike with. This will leave welts when swung with force, but will neither break bones nor maim. A concho belt used in this manner can draw blood. Anywhere on the body can be struck with an extended or doubled

strap, but strikes to the face and exposed flesh yield the best results. The belt is not wrapped around the hand for this technique—range is reduced by folding the belt in half (doubling) and striking with the extended midsection.

5. THE HORIZONTAL SWING: This is the most common attack, as it is simple and effective. The buckle is swung at the target along a straight horizontal plane, from either the outside or the inside, as hard as possible. The buckle will streak towards the target, impacting it with great force. The target can be struck repeatedly, in a rapid back and forth motion, incredibly fast—it is actually possible to strike an assailant four times in one second using this technique. The horizontal power-swing to the head is the most devastating move in beltfighting—a light belt can maim, and a heavy belt can kill.

Horizontal swings can be directed along declining planes, like targeting the rungs of a ladder. The uppermost rung would encompass the head of a standing opponent, the next lowest rung would be the shoulder and upper arm region, the rung beneath would be the elbows and extended hands, the rung beneath that would be the groin and lowered hands, and the bottommost rung would be the knee and shinbone region.

The buckle of a light belt will leave contusions and small lacerations, and the buckle of a heavy belt will do the same thing, only more severely—often cracking bone and ripping large gouges out of exposed flesh. If you miss with the buckle, the strap will impact your target and the buckle will wrap around, striking at reduced speed. It is imperative that you repeatedly practice striking targets at various distances until you gain familiarity with your weapon, otherwise, it will be far less effective in your hands. Pumpkins. melons, water jugs, and styrofoam heads all make excellent targets. It is possible (though unlikely) that the buckle may rebound at you, so be prepared to dodge if necessary.

6. THE SNAP: To do this, the belt can be held at your side or in front of you with the buckle hanging downwards. The belt can be fully extended, doubled, tripled, or (with thin belts) even concealed in the hand. Suddenly, with a flick of the wrist or quick movement of the lower arm, the buckle shoots directly towards your opponent in a straight line. As it impacts, it is immediately snapped back and readied once again.

This technique is primarily used to surprise and disorient an opponent. It has little risk of serious injury due to its low power, but is difficult to defend against. The primary targets are the face, hands, and groin. The snap takes time to perfect, but it is worth the effort—a master can repeatedly strike targets the size of a quarter, allowing him to pluck out an eye at will.

7. THE OVERHAND SWING: This can be a powerful attack, but it is easy to injure yourself if you miss. The belt comes up from behind you, over your head, and comes crashing down on your opponent at a high rate of speed. The primary target is the top of the head, though the face and hands can also be struck. If you overextend, the buckle will hit the back of his head at reduced speed. If you miss, you will need to sidestep to avoid inadvertently striking your knee or shin. If you crack your own shinbone, you will find yourself at a grave disadvantage. After sidestepping, you can redirect the belt to strike again. This move is dangerous, and requires hours of practice to perform safely.

8. THE UNDERHAND SWING: This is a good move because it is usually unexpected. The belt comes up from the floor behind you, swinging with increasing speed upwards into the target area. Targets include the groin, the hands, and the underside of the jaw. This is a difficult swing to master, primarily due to difficulties in targeting. The underhand swing is as dangerous as the overhand swing if you miss, due to the fact that you can inadvertently strike

yourself in the head. This swing takes hours of practice to perform safely.

9. DIAGONAL SWINGS: These are usually implemented without warning from the figure-8 pattern, which is suddenly greatly expanded as the attack is initiated. After you have mastered all the previous techniques, you can feel free to use diagonal attacks in combinations with horizontal and vertical ones. This gives you a great deal of versatility.

10. FANCY STUFF: In addition to smacking and slapping, the belt can also be used to trap, bind, block, throw, snag, and choke. These moves take years of practice to master, and are beyond the scope of this project. One technique that I will share is the simple block. To perform a block, the belt is grasped with both hands at shoulder length apart. There should be slack in the belt, allowing it to bang loosely between where it is grasped. To block a stick attack, the belt is suddenly raised into the proper position (either horizontal or vertical) and pulled taut. It will block almost as well as a rigid staff. With practice, the stick (or arm) can actually be trapped by wrapping the blocking belt around it and pulling in a spinning motion that will throw most assailants off balance. If you have mastered all the prior techniques and wish to learn more, consider obtaining some good books on *ninjutsu* (of which there are few—you'll need to be very selective). Be wary of unknown *"ninjutsu* masters" offering instruction, as becoming a ninja is a popular delusion among the freakishly deranged. If you feel you must attend classes, make sure your instructor is reputable.

Introduction to Knifefighting

Next to improvised bludgeons, knives are the most commonly encountered weapon on the streets. They are favored by people for a variety of reasons, but primarily due to their ease of access—if one does not happen to have a knife in one's pocket or on one's belt, a knife can simply be retrieved from any kitchen. Knives have contributed to most non-firearm related homicides, and the common kitchen knife is frequently cited as being the murder weapon.

Knives (particularly when long, sturdy, and sharp) are fearsome weapons. Simply grazing someone with the tip or edge is usually sufficient to split flesh and spill blood. Forceful chops and slashes can easily cut to the bone, severing any arteries, muscles, or nerves which might be in the way. And a powerful thrust will enable the blade to penetrate deep into body cavities, puncturing any organs therein and resulting in massive blood loss. It is relatively easy to inflict serious injuries upon the human body with a knife, even if one has no idea what one is doing (which, due to intoxication, mental illness, or simple ignorance, is often the case). Victims frequently die from knife wounds (either immediately, due to exsanguination and shock; or later, due to infection or other complications), even when their attacker did not intend to cause death. Knives can be extremely dangerous.

The majority of people who carry knives—even if their intent is to rely upon the knife for self-defense, do not know how to implement them as weapons other than "to poke someone with." While, in many cases, simply displaying a knife and showing willingness to use it may be sufficient to deter a lightweight threat (and most assailants would certainly reconsider the merits of continuing their attack after the first "poke"), an experienced streetfighter will *not* be impressed (indeed, he will most likely note your apparent lack of experience and attempt to use that to his advantage).

The intent of this section is not to "teach people how to kill with a knife" (as has been stated above, that is all too easy—even without instruction), but to share various tips which might better enable one to prevail in the unfortunate event that one is forced to rely upon cold steel to preserve life and limb.

1. Before choosing a knife as a weapon, ask yourself if you truly would be able to actually use it against another human being. This is not as simple as it might sound. The act of cutting another person (no matter what one's motivation might be) is considered repellant by our civilized society, and even if *you* do not have a problem with it, most policemen, judges, and juries would (not to mention the journalists, who would be sure to present you to the public as a bloodthirsty psychopath). Many gung- ho commando wannabes (as well as potential freaks) seem to think that sticking a knife in one's enemy would be pretty cool—it would definitely show everyone what a badass you truly believe yourself to be—however, they often have not thought things through.

    If you stab someone, they are going to bleed—a *lot*. You could very well find yourself drenched with the (possibly infectious) blood of another (not to mention ragged bits of meat). Blood is wet, sticky, highly visible, and it smells bad. If you are covered in blood, others will surely notice, and there is a minimal chance you'll be able to get away. If you really want to experience a hint of what it's like to stab another human being, I'd suggest volunteering to assist a farmer as he slaughters and butchers a hog. The resulting noise, stench, and mess to be cleaned up will give you a healthy dose of reality. It is ugly, brutal, and highly distasteful—but sometimes it needs to be done. The only people who "enjoy" this sort of thing are immature shitheads who've never done it (although they might claim otherwise), and perverted freaks who jerk off to slasher-porn while fantasizing about serial murder.

2. If you've decided to use a knife as a weapon, be sure to choose the longest, sturdiest, and pointiest one you can find (unless you intend to carry it concealed on a daily basis, in which case it would probably be best to favor a large folder which can be used for utilitarian purposes as well). The longer the blade is, the further your effective range will be, and the deeper you'll be able to penetrate. The seemingly insignificant difference between a 6" blade and an 8" blade will become readily apparent when engaging armed sparring partners (with dull training blades) or padded training targets (with live blades). Longer blades will also add more cutting surface to power slashes, and more mass to chops. They also appear more intimidating, and are better suited for keeping an attacker at a distance.

    In my opinion, when it comes to knives, anything with less than a 6" blade is bullshit. Sure, you can reach the heart (up under the sternum) with a 5" blade, and slice open a throat with a serrated 4" blade, but you're sacrificing effectiveness for the luxury of discrete carry. The only folding knife I can personally endorse for proper execution of these techniques is the *Vaquero Grande* from Cold Steel. If you're relying upon a 3" "tactical folder," or a 2" "neck knife" for personal defense, be sure you're free of any grandiose delusions about your "weapon's" capabilities. Sure, it is possible to kill a man with a small blade (eventually), and it is a hell of a lot better than using one's empty hands, but it won't be nearly as efficient as an adequate length of steel.

    Remember, the common butcher knife (which also includes the chef's knife and carving knife) is one of the deadliest knives in the world—on many different levels. Not only has it been used in more homicides than any other bladed weapon, but it is typically longer, sturdier, and sharper than any flea market dagger or "combat/survival" knife. The width of the blade will create a large wound channel, and also forms an integral hilt (which will prevent your fingers from slipping over the edge upon thrusting into bone). Since the butcher knife can be found in virtually any household, you should familiarize yourself with it through extensive practice. If you want to rely upon a butcher knife for home defense, I recommend wrapping the grip with friction tape to reduce the likelihood of slippage.

3. Make sure that your blade is kept *sharp*. Either learn how to use a whetstone, invest in a top quality knife sharpening system, or purchase an electric sharpener for the best possible edge. If you are too inept to use a whetstone, or too poor to obtain a proper sharpener, at the very least pick up one of those crossed-hone style sharpening devices commonly found at gun shows. Most of the hones and sharpeners found in department stores are woefully inadequate. Some steels, like cheap stainless, are difficult to sharpen and don't hold an edge—they seem to go dull just from sitting in their sheaths! Your knife needs to be able to inflict clean deep cuts on layers of corrugated cardboard, tough cuts of raw meat, and rolled carpet remnants. Your blade doesn't need to be able to split hairs, but it *should* be able to slice through a leather jacket or sever a free-hanging length of inch-thick hemp rope. From my own observations, the majority of knives carried on the street are either partially or completely dull. This will usually be the case unless the owner has used knives extensively (such as for camping or food preparation) and knows how to take proper care of them.

4. Don't lose your balance or leave yourself open. Many inexperienced knifefighters over-extend themselves on their thrusts, over-commit themselves to a specific technique, or forget to guard their vital areas. They may focus only on using the knife, forgetting completely about their other hand, elbows, and feet. Missed slashes may follow through too far. A downward stab which misses might

even result in a wound to the top of one's thigh! Many hours of practice (against imaginary opponents, against practice targets, against sparring partners, and in front of a mirror) will be necessary in order to attain a reasonable level of competence.

5. NEVER DROP YOUR KNIFE!!! This is easier said than done. Often, a knife will be immediately dropped upon drawing, simply because one is overly nervous and is more concerned about drawing the knife quickly rather than securing a firm grip. If your knife has a smooth handle which becomes slippery with sweat (or blood), it can fall from your grasp. For this reason, a textured grip (like stag or Kraton) is recommended—or you could wear thin, leather, fingerless gloves. If your grip is not secure (like the "commando" and "saber" grips, which require one to press one's thumb against the side of the handle, rather than wrapping around it), the knife can easily be wrenched from your grasp upon solid contact with bone (or a sturdy training target). If the knuckles or wrist of your knife hand are struck or cut, you could easily lose your grip. Be extremely careful when switching grips (and do not attempt to do so unless you've first devoted hours to switching grips in training), and *never* toss your knife up in the air to switch grips! Your knife should never become airborne. If you need to switch hands, carefully pass it from one hand to the other—do not toss it from hand to hand! Always keep a solid grip on the handle, with your thumb wrapped securely around it (rather than pressed to the side or placed atop the pommel).

6. Use the entire knife. Not only can the blade be used to stab, slash, and chop, but the tip (particularly with a clip point blade) can be used to rip (this is often done when one's knife arm is grasped at the wrist by an opponent). The pommel can be used to hammer with, to great effect (and many pommels are specially designed to make them more effective in this capacity). On larger fighting knives (like bowies and medieval daggers), the quillion (hilt) can

be used to block, trap, or even break the blade of an attacker's knife. With heavy bladed knives, the unsharpened spine of the blade (as well as the flat) can be used to either parry or bludgeon.

7. Practice extensively. If you intend to rely upon a knife for self-defense purposes, you need to know exactly what your effective range is, as well as the best methods of executing slashes to various targets—this knowledge can only be acquired through experience. All practice techniques must first be performed correctly at low speed before attempting to execute them quickly! Failure to abide by this simple guideline will result in sloppy technique, as well as possible injury!

First, one must begin the boring and repetitive process of learning to draw one's knife quickly, without snagging it on clothing (or the sheath's retention snap, if applicable) or dropping it. After having mastered drawing (and resheathing) your knife, one can then practice implementing simple horizontal slashes at varying levels. Spend at least an hour doing nothing but horizontal slashes (both fore and backhand) at face, throat, stomach, groin, and knee level (visualize the rungs of a ladder). Next, one can practice various diagonal and vertical slashes and chops.

After one has the general concept of slashing down, one can begin practicing straight thrusts and uppercuts (but *not* downward stabs). Be sure not to over-extend yourself or lose your balance! In my opinion, one of the best techniques for delivering a straight-line attack to the throat or solar plexus area is the "pronated thrust," which is delivered by first cocking back the shoulder, then twisting the arm as it shoots forward, so that the blade is being held horizontally as it enters the imaginary target. BE SURE YOU'RE HOLDING THE KNIFE CORRECTLY! The blade should be extending from the top of your hand (edge facing down), with your thumb wrapped around the grip—this is commonly referred to as the "natural," or "hammer" grip. Once you've done a hundred or so stabbing movements, you can practice combination attacks versus an imaginary opponent (with a reasonable expectation that you will not inadvertently injure yourself). Only after you are comfortable with drawing your knife and launching combination attacks should you consider practicing with the "icepick grip" (in which the blade protrudes from the bottom of one's fist, with the edge facing outwards). This is considered to be a somewhat advanced technique, in that not only must one be at extremely close range to use it effectively, but one can easily injure oneself or become disarmed if it is utilized incorrectly. Although it is extremely versatile and provides for superior penetration, the icepick grip is definitely not for everyone, and many experts have advised against using it. If you would like to practice with this grip, be aware that it has many limitations (lack of range, ease of being blocked, danger to self), however, it is many knifefighters' grip of choice when confronting an unarmed opponent (who will probably attempt to immediately close into grappling range). If you decide that the grip has merit, you'll need to practice switching grips one-handed—this is not as easy as it sounds. The handle must be able to be reversed in one's hand, in under a second, by moving the fingers only slightly—you will need to practice this over a hundred times before the movement becomes ingrained into one's "muscle memory" (so it can be performed automatically, with smoothness and precision).

After you've mastered defeating an imaginary opponent (a mirror will help you to correct sloppy movements), you can construct a variety of targets to practice with. Targets are very important, because they not only show you how little range you actually have to work with, but they will improve accuracy and show you the limitations of your particular knife. There are numerous subtle variations on slashing with a knife (such as grazing, slapping, dragging, hooking, etc.), all of which can produce cuts of different lengths and depths. You will need to experiment extensively in order to find out what methods work best for you.

Targets can be constructed of nearly anything (just try to avoid using materials, such as nails or metal tubing, which might chip the edge of your blade). Cardboard cartons, large melons, and sides of beef have all been used for practicing blade techniques. An adequate target for introductory use would be several layers of corrugated cardboard rectangles (1' X 2') bound together with duct tape and secured to a 2" X 4" set deep into the ground. After you've practiced extensively on numerous cardboard targets, you might consider constructing a scarecrow frame out of wood or PVC pipe, covering it with cloth or foam padding, then pulling a shirt and jacket over it. Some jacket materials, like denim and leather, are tough to defeat and serve as light armor. Due to the fact that denim and leather jackets are so commonly worn, it is important to know exactly what effect your knife will have against them. Be warned—if your grip isn't rock solid, you could easily find your fingers sliding over the blade after executing a hard thrust (especially with a hiltless weapon, like a small boot knife, a tactical folder, or a *balisong*)!

8. NEVER THROW YOUR KNIFE!!! It probably will not stick, and can easily be deflected or dodged. Once you've thrown your knife away, it will be unlikely that you'll have opportunity to retrieve it—although your opponent might choose to do so!

    There is one possible exception to this rule. With a large, heavy-bladed knife (like a butcher or Bowie knife), it is possible (after extensive practice) to implement a technique known as the "underhand chuck," by which the blade is tossed underhand (after gripping the handle) into the solar plexus area of an opponent standing within 5 feet of your extended arm. This is the *only* method of knife throwing that has any realistic combat application, but it would only prove useful in extremely rare instances.

9. Be aware of the knife's limitations. It is a very short range weapon, and should not be relied upon if you're facing a gun, bat, pool cue, chain, belt, or similar weapon. The only way you'd be able to even up the odds would be to either pick up an extended range weapon yourself, or to immediately close with your opponent (making it difficult for him to swing his weapon or get off a shot).

10. Decide in advance if your intent will be to kill, disable, or repel (as each goal requires specific targeting). If you simply want to dissuade, chase off, or escape from a significantly larger assailant, simply slashing at his forehead, hands, and wrists (or even feigning to do so) will usually be sufficient (and have little risk of inadvertently inflicting serious injury).

    If your assailant is armed, but you would still like to avoid killing him, it may be possible to disarm him by attacking his weapon arm. The fingers (or thumb) could be hacked at, or the tendons in the back of the hand could be cut with a powerslash. A deep slice anywhere on the wrist or forearm could result in profuse bleeding and loss of mobility—the inside of the elbow is an excellent target as well. A thrust or powerslash to the muscles of the upper arm (biceps, triceps, or deltoid) can also result in loss of mobility (although to a lesser extent, unless a large blade is being used). A deep stab into the underarm can be lethal, so this target should be avoided. In my opinion, the best way to disarm an assailant would be to forcefully stab your blade completely through his forearm (between the ulna and radius—best accomplished by stabbing the inside surface of the lower wrist), then twisting it before retraction. Be advised, however, that these disarming techniques are far from harmless, and could very well result in permanent paralysis.

    If you feel that you are in significant danger of being crippled or maimed (as when facing an extremely vicious attacker, or multiple opponents), you will want to slash, chop, or stab deep into your opponent's arms and legs, in hopes of severing muscles, tendons, arteries, and nerves. Hard slashes to the face, chest, and abdomen might also be appropriate. Remember, there are many ways to make any given cut.

If, however, you are facing an unusually determined (or criminally psychotic) attacker, it may become necessary to actually "take him out." This can be done in a variety of ways. Although the head or chest can be pierced with a stout blade held in the "icepick grip," it is far more likely that it will be deflected by bone—and in the event that it *does* penetrate, it will surely be wedged firmly in place. Although the head and chest *are* considered to be vital areas, softer tissues would prove more vulnerable. The throat (trachea, carotid arteries, jugular veins) is an excellent target for a stab or power-slash, as is the side of the neck. There are several ways to execute a "powerslash," but the easiest way to describe this method of attack is simply: to chop full-force into the opponent's neck before draw-ing the edge across hard and deep—speed of execution should be approximately 1/4 second.

The subclavian artery can be severed by stabbing one's blade deep into the target's shoulder (between the clavicle and scapula) and forcefully pumping the handle. If the kidney is stabbed into (and the handle pumped, as above), the renal artery can be severed. After a "pumped stab" has been delivered, be sure to twist the blade prior to extraction, thereby enlarging the wound channel and maximizing drainage. By jamming the blade up deep under-neath the sternum, one can pierce the heart or sever the abdominal aorta. Any one of these vulnerable areas could be targeted for a mortal wound, with death occurring within minutes.

11. Accept that you are going to be hurt—probably seriously. If the other guy also has a knife (regardless of his skill level), *you will get cut!* Even if the other guy(s) is unarmed, he will start to claw, gouge, and bite immediately after the knife goes in. If he sees the knife before you have opportunity to cut him—and decides to stay

and fight nonetheless—switch into "full combat mode," because you've got a serious situation on your hands! The presence of a weapon (particularly a knife) takes the conflict to a whole new level, and a guy who might've just wanted to "have a little fun" (by kicking your ass) will suddenly start looking for a proper cudgel with which to splatter your brains. Then, there is always the possibility that, in the midst of a struggle, you could accidentally cut or stab *yourself* (not uncommon).

12. Expect to go to jail. At the very least, you could be charged with weapon possession and "menacing." If your assailant is cut—however slightly—you will be charged with felonious assault (or "assault with a deadly weapon"). Other charges could include attempted murder, manslaughter, and homicide. You might very well have a legitimate claim to self-defense (as well as a clean record), but consider what a jury of typical sheeplike citizens might think when the prosecutor shows them the knife you used, along with a series of large color photographs of the "victim's" wounds—then proceeds to state that you must've been "looking for trouble" due to the fact that you were carrying the "big scary fighting knife" *concealed on your person!* He'll make you appear to be some sort of depraved monster, whom the frightened jury members will literally *beg* to have locked safely away forever. Unfair? Perhaps, but that is exactly what's going to happen. If you cut someone with a knife, no matter how justified you might've been in doing so, you will probably do time as a result.

I hope that you've learned something from this section. There are a lot of near- bloodless knifefights in countless action movies, and manufacturers of "tactical knives" tend to advertise heavily at the "macho-man" market, but knifefighting cannot by any stretch of the imagination be considered glamourous. Stabbing another human being is a horribly brutal act, and if you happen to do so, society will think that you're a fearsome monster who needs to be locked in a cage. Knifefighting is not an "art," nor is it something that will make you a better person in any way—it is simply a survival skill, to become familiar with in hopes that you will never actually need to rely upon it.

Handguns

The subject of handguns has been addressed, in detail, by a vast number of authors. Thousands of essays have been penned regarding: gun rights, gun safety, gun handling, marksmanship, defensive shooting, concealed carry, ammunition types, opinions on the quality of various handguns, and many related topics. You could literally fill a small library with what has been published on these subjects. This section is intended to provide a concise introduction to the subject for the uninformed, and has deliberately been kept brief. If handguns interest you, further study and professional instruction is strongly recommended.

INTRODUCTION:

By far, the deadliest (hence most effective) weapon one can have on one's person is a firearm. A firearm can intimidate, wound, or kill from a considerable distance with only the light exertion of a single digit. Compact lightweight firearms, designed to be worn in a holster or dropped in a pocket, are commonly referred to as "handguns." Because of their small size, they tend to be far less powerful than the average rifle or shotgun. Most handguns have minimal "stopping power," but still tend to inflict more damage than would a knife or club while requiring far less skill, effort, and commitment to implement effectively.

The negatives of carrying a handgun are that, not only is possession and use strictly regulated in most jurisdictions, but it is far too easy to accidentally injure or kill innocent bystanders—even those who might be unseen in a building across the street! Furthermore, the only purpose the defensive handgun serves is to *kill*…it cannot be relied upon to simply threaten or incapacitate. If you choose to secrete a handgun upon your person with which to defend yourself, you must do so with a complete understanding of the awesome responsibility you have undertaken.

Handguns generally fall into one of three categories: revolver, autoloading pistol, and "other." The latter category would include derringers, manually operated repeaters, single shot handguns, muzzleloaders, and various exotic weapons such as penguns and "stingers." In this section, we will discuss only the first two categories.

Experts usually agree that the following factors must be taken into consideration when choosing a defensive handgun: reliability, effectiveness, accuracy, and concealability (however, concealability would not be a factor if your handgun will remain in your nightstand or glovebox). We shall examine each of these factors now.

RELIABILITY:

A defensive firearm must be counted upon to instantly fire a potentially lethal projectile upon each and every squeeze of the trigger. A weapon which tends to jam, or otherwise fail to operate as intended, is worse than useless. There is nothing more disheartening than hearing an innocuous *click* when one is anticipating a deafening report. Most well-maintained quality firearms loaded with fresh ammunition can be relied upon after a hundred practice rounds have been fired without a single jam. Poor quality ammunition and defective magazines are the cause of most jams.

EFFECTIVENESS:

A defensive firearm must be counted upon to stop a determined assailant with no more than two shots to the center of mass. Due to the ballistic inferiority of most handgun calibers, very few sidearms will meet this criteria. However, some calibers are less inferior than others. Acceptable calibers include (but are not limited to): .22 Winchester

Magnum Rimfire, .32 H&R Magnum, .357 Magnum, .357 SIG, .40 S&W, and .45 ACP. Many firearms experts will disagree with my choice of the .22 WMR, and will note that I failed to include the .38 Special, .44 Special, 9mm, and heavier magnum cartridges. I have my reasons for this, which I will address later. Let it suffice to say that, whatever your choice of caliber, it must neither be too low powered to be ineffective, nor so high powered as to prevent accurate rapid firing.

ACCURACY:

While it is known that in the vast majority of incidents where a handgun was used defensively ranges seldom exceeded ten feet, it is comforting to have the ability to precisely deliver an aimed long range shot if required. Any handgun intended for defensive use (excepting derringers) must be able to place every round fired within a five-inch diameter circle from thirty feet away...even an amateur can accomplish this with a minimum of dedication and practice. A miniaturized laser designator can be affixed to the triggerguard (or mounted elsewhere on the weapon) to increase speed and confidence. A poor quality handgun with a loose mechanism or worn out barrel may fire unacceptably large groupings, or even allow bullets to tumble as they exit the bore, rather than flying true.

CONCEALABILITY:

If one intends to carry a sidearm, it must be done discreetly...people tend to get rather nervous upon seeing a stranger in possession of a loaded firearm walking about in public (unless a police badge is plainly visible). If a weapon is to be carried regularly, it must be compact and lightweight—eliminating most long-barreled magnums and "super-automatics." Furthermore, a top quality holster should be selected to ensure comfort and eliminate unsightly (and suspicious) bulges.

OTHER CONSIDERATIONS:

Your sidearm should feel comfortable in your hand. The grip should not be so large you cannot close your hand around it, nor should it be awkwardly angled. The stocks should neither be so rough as to abrade the hand, nor so smooth as to slip within one's grasp (stag and textured rubber are good choices). Blued steel or brushed stainless are both far better finishes than highly reflective nickel plate (though opinions differ on this). Your primary sidearm must be a weapon that you trust, feel comfortable with, and would be proud to display. When your life may depend on your choice of tool, it is foolish to choose that tool lightly. Research your potential choices carefully, and don't scrimp on quality to save a buck. The sidearm you select will be your primary talisman of protection for many years.

REVOLVERS:

The two basic categories of revolver are single-action and double-action. The hammer of a single-action revolver must be physically cocked back prior to each and every shot, and must be carefully de-cocked if one decides not to fire. These are typically modern reproductions of antique six-shooters chambered for commercial ammunition rather than "cap and ball." With the exception of the fine North American Arms mini-revolvers chambered for .22 WMR, these mostly include long-barreled monstrosities chambering powerful loads which are unsuitable for concealed carry.

Double-action revolvers will fire each time the trigger is squoze, and can also be manually cocked to fire a carefully aimed shot with minimal trigger pull—this style is most commonly seen. Occasionally seen nowadays is the "double-action only" revolver (typically a snubbie) which cannot be manually cocked—this bit of "idiot- proofing" is a safety mechanism intended to lessen the likelihood of an accidental discharge—such guns are intended for use by persons unfamiliar with firearms, and are not recommended.

Revolvers are simple to understand, have no safety switches to mess with, and rarely jam—which makes them the ideal choice for the novice. I would recommend a barrel length of at least two inches, but no more than four inches, without porting (a recoil moderating vent which impairs night vision when firing).

AUTOLOADING PISTOLS:

You should not purchase a pistol unless you are willing to devote many hours towards gaining proficiency. You need to be experienced at clearing jams, changing magazines, and stripping down your weapon for cleaning. I will not discuss pistols further except to say that if you are such a fumble-fingered dunce as to require a DAO (double-action only) version, you cannot be expected to clear jams, reload rapidly, or maintain your weapon—stick to a revolver instead. Automatics are for expert pistoleros so intimately familiar with their weapon that they can double-tap multiple targets in low light conditions without using their sights—and never miss a shot. A novice with an automatic pistol and no instructor to correct his mistakes is an accident waiting to happen.

APOLOGIA:

Here I shall explain my rationale for caliber selection. The .22 WMR's penetration and destructive power has been understated or ignored by many experts (who should know better). This, combined with its light recoil, makes it ideal for small framed novices. The .22 LR, .25 ACP , .32 ACP, and .32 S&W Long are all too weak to be relied upon. Many people believe the .32 H&R Magnum to be a superior round to the .38 SPL, and it too has a relatively light recoil. The .38 SPL has been proven to be ineffective when fired from a short barrel unless loaded to "+P" pressures, which many guns cannot safely withstand. The .380 ACP and 9mm rounds, especially when loaded with FMJ Ball, have both shown poor stopping power. The .44 Special initially appears to be a satisfactory choice, but has shown poor performance in the field when fired from the typical 5-shot snubbie.

The .357 Magnum is the heaviest cartridge most people would feel comfortable firing, and a novice could load it with .38 SPL +P for reduced recoil. The .357 SIG has a bottlenecked casing for reduced likelihood of a "failure to feed" jam, and has shown good performance when quality hollowpoints are used (however, many shooters feel that it recoils too hard for accurate rapid firing). The .40 S&W and .45 ACP have both shown adequate performance, and are relied upon by most police officers. Rounds like the .41 Magnum, .44 Magnum, .45 Long Colt, .454 Casull, and .50 Action Express not only deliver punishing recoil, but require a weapon of such size and weight as to be impractical for concealed carry.

Two handguns of differing calibers which I feel are worthy of mention are the Walther TPH (and the similarly styled Iver Johnson TP-22) and the Tokerov. The TPH and TP-22 are compact double-action pistols chambered for the inexpensive .22 Long Rifle cartridge which, when hyper-velocity rounds like the CCI Stinger or Quik Shok are used, have proven far more effective than either the .25 ACP or .32 ACP—both popular chamberings for diminutive pocket pistols. The Tokerov is a military automatic designed by the Soviets and used extensively throughout the world. It is a single-action with no safety mechanisms, so the hammer must be physically cocked back prior to firing the first shot, after which the movement of the slide will automatically cock the hammer for subsequent shots. The powerful round (comparable to the .38 Super Automatic) it fires has a bottlenecked casing like the much newer .357 SIG, making it less prone to jamming. A used Tokerov in very good condition can be purchased for approximately one hundred dollars—a fraction of what a used Colt or Beretta will cost you.

AMMUNITION:

There are dozens of different types of ammunition available for most calibers. The most commonly seen include: ball, softpoint, hollowpoint, and prefragmented. Ball ammunition has a lead projectile with a full metal jacket for easy feeding in autoloaders. It is the cheapest and most common round. It tends not to deform, resulting in overpenetration and minimal stopping power. It is best suited for target practice. Softpoint ammunition has a jacketed lead projectile with exposed lead at the tip, allowing the bullet to partially flatten (mushroom) upon impact, transferring more energy to the target and enlarging the wound channel. It is a little better than ball ammunition, but not as effective as hollowpoints.

Hollowpoint ammunition has a jacketed or semi-jacketed lead projectile with a hole drilled into the tip. Hollowpoints are designed to mushroom or break apart upon striking a target, resulting in increased destructiveness. Premium hollowpoints may have specially designed cavities or pre-segmented projectiles in addition to an increased powder charge, resulting in maximum expansion—they are the defensive ammo of choice.

The bullet projectile of prefragmented ammunition typically consists of small lead pellets packed within a metallic shell, which effectively explodes upon contact. These rounds do an incredible amount of damage, and as a bonus will not overpenetrate targets or pass through walls. Their downside is that they are incredibly expensive and may break apart inside heavy clothing. Glaser Safety Slugs and BeeSafe rounds can be found at better gun stores or special ordered.

Other types of projectiles include: soft lead bullets, which are obsolete; wadcutters, which are low-powered cylindrical projectiles used for target practice; semi-wadcutters, which are truncated soft lead projectiles often recommended for use in airweight snubbies; shotshells, which fire a cloud of small pellets out the muzzle of your handgun, and are good for dispatching snakes or chasing off unmotivated lightweight goblins; tracers, which are ball ammunition treated with phosphorous, which burns to create a bright trail behind each projectile; exploders, which contain a small explosive charge that seldom detonates, and is vastly overrated as well as prohibited in many jurisdictions; and blank cartridges, which have no projectile and often jam in autoloaders.

GUN SAFETY:

Much has been written on this subject, but I will touch on the basics here:

1. Be familiar with your firearm. Read the owner's manual. Learn all aspects of loading, unloading, firing, decocking, disassembling, and cleaning before even *thinking* about loading it with live ammunition. Firearms are dangerous, and can accidentally discharge if mishandled. Anything (or anyone) in front of the muzzle will experience destruction as a bullet passes through.

2. Always assume that any firearm you encounter is loaded—even if you are told otherwise.

3. Never point the muzzle of a firearm at anything you do not wish to immediately kill or destroy.

4. Keep your finger outside of the triggerguard until just prior to the moment you are about to fire.

5. Never practice with, clean, or otherwise handle firearms if your ability or judgement is in any way impaired (such as by intoxicants, distractions, or strong emotions).

6. Never allow your firearm to be handled by a child or irresponsible adult—this may entail keeping it locked in a drawer while you are absent.

7. If you must fire your weapon, whether in practice or actual combat, ascertain that there is a suitable backstop present to prevent missed or overpenetrated rounds from being a hazard to others.

8. If you are a drunk or an idiot, you have no business owning a firearm.

LEGALITIES:

The laws regarding individual ownership of firearms vary greatly from place to place, and it is *imperative* that you are fully knowledgeable of the laws pertaining to your jurisdiction (as well as other jurisdictions you commonly travel through). Some states have almost no restrictions on firearm ownership, other states either require pistol permits or prohibit concealed carry, and in some places (like New York) it is actually a *felony* for a law-abiding citizen with no criminal record to own an unlicenced handgun (this even applies to residents of neighboring states briefly crossing the border with a legally owned handgun in their vehicle).

Not only does your right to own a firearm change depending on what state you happen to be in, but the level of force permissible to defend oneself varies as well. Usually, lethal force can be used only when yourself or a relation is in the process of being attacked by an assailant that can reasonably be construed as having the means to immediately kill you (such as when you are being charged by an individual brandishing a butcher knife, whereas if the same individual were merely brandishing said knife from a distance of 30 feet, you would not be considered to be "imperiled" under the law as written). In most places, lethal force cannot be applied to a "fleeing felon" or in defense of one's property. In some localities, a criminal who breaks into your home and assaults you is entitled to file a lawsuit against you for injuries received due to "excessive use of force" on your part!

Even if you are completely justified in using deadly force to protect yourself and your family, if you inadvertently violate one of the hundreds of statutes pertaining to weapon ownership or self-defense, you can reasonably expect to be convicted and incarcerated—do not assume that a misinformed and disinterested "jury of one's peers" will automatically acquit you after having been bullied by the prosecution into thinking they have "no other choice but to convict." Go to the public library or use the Internet to research these laws—if you decide to ask the police or a government clerk about them you could find yourself the subject of unwanted scrutiny. If you violate the law and are caught, ignorance is no excuse.

Federal legislation has effectively nullified the 2nd amendment, so it cannot be called upon to overrule unjust laws believed to be unconstitutional. Learn what actions are prohibited by your state's bureaucrats, or risk punishment for running afoul of an unknown regulation. The government enforces these laws zealously, but puts a very low priority on educating the public about them. If you want to reduce your chances of being victimized by the "justice system" it is your responsibility to educate yourself. If you own a gun for protection, ignorance of the law can become a huge liability.

DEFENDING YOURSELF:

This is an extremely serious situation—a "worst case scenario," if you will, and every situation is different. I will now give the uninformed a few tips on how to go about using one's handgun as an effective weapon. Opinions vary, and many experts may disagree with my advice.

1. If you have not practiced quickdrawing your weapon, now is not a good time to start. Using your weak hand to push away an assailant, step back and calmly draw your weapon in a single fluid motion. Adrenaline may hamper manual dexterity, so be careful not to drop it.

2. It is best to use your sights, if feasible. If you attempt to "shoot from the hip" (without benefit of extensive practice) you will probably miss...even at relatively close range. Installing a laser designator on your weapon can give you a significant edge.

3. It is best to grasp the weapon with both hands. Cup your dominant hand with your weak hand—do not grasp the wrist. It is best not to lock your elbows. Keep your knees slightly bent, and do not lose your balance.

4. Do not draw your weapon unless you intend to fire it. If you are uncomfortable with the concept of blasting holes in an attacker at point blank range, and quite possibly getting showered with gore in the process, you will hesitate and may very well be overpowered and have your own weapon turned against you. If there is any doubt in your mind about whether you could actually shoot an assailant, you should leave your gun at home and carry pepperspray instead.

   This is neither weakness or cowardice, but common sense—if you are unsure how you would react when confronted by the goblins (who will generally attempt to appear non-threatening at first, so as to take you off-guard), then a concealed handgun might well be more of a detriment than an asset. Most people, however, would not hesitate to give an assailant a faceful of pepperspray when use of a firearm might be deemed inappropriate.

   Remember, a gun is not a "magic wand" that will automatically frighten and intimidate everyone when brandished...many inexperienced citizens in the midst of an adrenal dump have "frozen up" upon being confronted with a goblin who refused to listen to them. If you freeze due to "brain lock" or a bad reaction to the unfamiliar effects of adrenaline, the goblin will be able to take full advantage of the situation—victimizing you and getting a new gun in the process. DO NOT CARRY A HANDGUN UNLESS YOU ARE WILLING TO USE IT!

5. If you have opportunity, and your attacker hesitates upon seeing your weapon, you should command him to stop his activities and immediately leave the area. If you are a novice, you should not attempt an apprehension unless absolutely necessary. Do not expect to be treated like a "hero" by either the police or the news media, as that would be highly unlikely—indeed, expect to be treated like a criminal yourself. Many criminals are desperate individuals who will avoid incarceration through any means necessary. Some might require a daily ration of drugs, others might be looking at spending the rest of their lives in prison due to being repeat violent offenders, and a few might fear being killed by other prisoners for being a known snitch—and here you are, all pale and trembling, saying, "Put your hands on your head—I'm calling the police!" Many criminals will willingly risk death in order to get away, and unless you are an expert *pistolero* with a background in law enforcement, it is generally best to let them. If you point a gun at a goblin and tell him to "Piss off," he generally will be more than happy to oblige, and will seldom hold a grudge. If you are a novice gun handler, and no-ne has been raped or murdered, NEVER ATTEMPT TO APPREHEND A CRIMINAL YOURSELF! The risks far outweigh the potential benefits.

6. If your attacker advances, becomes argumentative, attempts to distract you, or says something like "you won't shoot me" or "that gun's not loaded," he is attempting to divert your attention from the fact that he is about to charge you! Immediately fire two rounds into him without hesitation. If you have given him an opportunity to depart, and he instead chooses to take the chance that you won't be able to shoot him before he gets you, then you are dealing with an extremely dangerous predator who deserves to die. This is not to be considered a "pre-emptive strike," as his

attack has already commenced. Of course, it will be necessary to fib and say simply that "he was attacking me" if you want to avoid life imprisonment for depriving the poor misunderstood deviant of his freedom of speech.

However, in the event that you are able to remain calm in such a situation, it may not be necessary to kill unnecessarily. Instead, you could simply cock back the hammer of your weapon and say, plainly and slowly, "If you do not leave now, you are going to die." Some insane individuals who truly do not care if they die, and might well be harboring suicidal tendencies, might reconsider their actions if you took careful aim at their pecker and asked if they wanted to be deprived of it. If you are a good shot (and no-one is downstairs), you might consider firing a "warning shot" directly into the top of his foot…the chances that he will be killed are minimal, and the blood trail will make it easy for the police to track him.

7. Never allow any suspect individual to come within ten feet of you if you have a gun in your hand. Watch their hands to ascertain they're not going for a concealed weapon. If you can't see their hands, or if they make a furtive motion, immediately call them on it. If he is obviously drawing a weapon, immediately shoot him twice in the chest, then step back to ascertain that you can see both hands. If you cannot, and he appears to be attempting to continue his attack (after being warned to do otherwise), shoot him again—in the head, if possible.

8. Never believe anything a goblin tells you.

9. Never surrender your weapon under any circumstances (except to a uniformed police officer responding to the disturbance). If a loved one is being threatened, I'd advise taking the chance and shooting the goblin, whether your loved one is in the line of fire or not, if they have been promised safe passage upon letting your

loved one go, but still insist you give them your weapon. If you find yourself wrestling for the weapon (which never would've happened if you'd kept him at a distance and didn't let anyone sneak up on you from behind), shoot him if possible. Bite, gouge, and (if you have a knife) stab, but *do not let go of that weapon!* If you think you are going to be overpowered and have the weapon taken from you, despite all your efforts to prevent it, try to temporarily decommission it (either by removing the magazine or dumping the contents of the cylinder).

10. If you must fire your weapon, aim for the center of mass (upper torso), and be careful not to inadvertently fire all your bullets—especially if there are multiple assailants. Keep track of how many rounds you've fired (to the best of your ability), even if you need to count aloud. If engaging multiple armed assailants, it is recommended that one reload (behind adequate cover) prior to emptying one's weapon.

11. If the police show up, immediately holster your weapon, show your empty hands, and identify yourself. Follow all of their instructions precisely. If they ask you to place your weapon on the ground, do so without argument. Expect to have guns pointed at you before being handcuffed and searched. If you approach them with a gun in your hand, it is possible you will be shot. After explaining the basics of what happened, immediately request to speak with your attorney if their questions become too intrusive. If you are at home, they will probably want to enter your home to "take a look around." Expect to be arrested and charged with homicide (or whatever charge is applicable).

AFTERWORD:

A handgun, should you choose to own and carry one (and they are most definitely not for everyone) must not only be reliable as well as powerful, but you must feel comfortable with it on many different levels. It must be loaded with the finest quality ammunition you can acquire. The center of mass (upper torso) should be your target of choice, as a bobbing and weaving head is far too difficult a shot for anyone but a true expert. Your weapon must be properly cleaned after each use, and must be protected from lint and moisture. The handgun requires far more practice than the rifle if proficiency is to be attained, as well as maintained. The handgun has enormous capacity for destruction, and has no business in the hands of the irresponsible or the inept.

If you carry a handgun for defensive purposes, that is not a fact you want to be broadcasting publicly—indeed, it might be best not to let anyone know that you even *own* a gun, as they might see fit to blab about it to others. Not only has the media so demonized law abiding gun owners that they are now commonly thought of as dangerously unstable, but criminally minded people might be tempted to abscond with your weapon, and a particularly devious enemy might use knowledge of your gun ownership as a means to discredit or wrongfully prosecute you—keep your weapon a closely guarded secret!

Being a gun owner is a great responsibility with a significant potential for abuse. If you believe that you, or someone else in your household, might be capable of abusing a firearm, it is best not to tempt fate. Firearms are not for everyone, but for those who are comfortable with them, they provide a sense of security and empowerment unlike anything else. There are many good things to be said about a device that enables a frail or elderly individual to vanquish a physically superior criminal deviate (or deviates) intent on victimizing them. Nothing can protect you and your family better than a quality firearm.

Primitive Weapons for Home Defense

L ike most warriors, I am of the opinion that a firearm is unsurpassed in the realm of both personal and home defense. A highly tuned Colt-style .45 ACP (or a *SIG-Sauer* chambered for the bottle-necked .357 SIG cartridge) is the best choice for a competent *pistolero* to carry on his person (a short-barreled wheelgun chambered for .32 H&R magnum or .357 magnum (loaded with .38 SPL +P ammunition) is best for the novice). A laser-equipped magnum revolver capable of stopping an automobile is the best choice for concealing in one's vehicle. A short-barreled autoloading shotgun equipped with a tactical light and loaded with #1 Buck is the best choice for laying aside one's bed. These opinions are shared by the majority of experts in the field.

However, I realize that owning a firearm is not an option for many people. Some warriors I have known have a strong aversion to firearms. These people usually are either classical martial artists or regular participants at the Renaissance Fairs, although some may have had a bad experience with firearms in the past. Other people are prohibited by law from owning firearms, either because they live in a Draconian jurisdiction that has outlawed guns, or because they've violated the law in the past. Most law-breakers are scumbags, but many decent citizens have wrongfully been convicted of a crime (such as assault, weapon possession, marijuana possession, or other such minor violations carrying severe penalties) in their youth and have been unable to eliminate the stigma of a criminal conviction from their record. Other people may live in a densely populated area, such as an apartment complex or

113

trailer park, where firing a weapon at an assailant would constitute reckless endangerment.

It is always preferable to fight with a weapon than without, especially when attacked by a stranger in your home or when confronting a group of potential assailants. Many primitive weapons will serve quite well in this capacity. This list has been compiled of effective and reliable weapons ideal for use in close quarters. The weapons are classified by type, and their various attributes are commented upon. These weapons are, for the most part, not of an improvised nature and must be secured beforehand for the purpose of defense. Some, such as martial-arts weapons and modified tools, are illegal to possess in many jurisdictions. While some may think this listing incomplete, we have deliberately chosen to disregard many people's "favorites" for reasons of practicality and conciseness.

THE LONG KNIFE:

The world's deadliest weapon, used in more homicides and armed assaults than any other, is the humble kitchen knife.

Long Bowie knives are often well made, but start at over a hundred dollars. Long bladed "survival" or "combat" knives are generally poorly designed, overpriced, and shoddily constructed from inferior materials. Top quality fighting knives often exceed two hundred dollars, and tend to be intended more for display purposes than actual use. A good quality butcher or chef knife can be had at any department store for under $15 (don't waste your money on a flimsy $5 supermarket knife). Top quality meatcutting knives, often with up to 18" blades, start at around $40 and are a good investment for home defense due to their keen edge and extended reach.

Butcher and Chef knives often have blade lengths between 8" and 12", are made from quality steel designed to take and hold an edge, and can be legally owned by anyone (provided it is not carried concealed). They are found in most homes, and are a far better choice than the majority of "fighting knives" offered for sale. The knife should be thick and heavy—it needs to be substantial to hack with. The handle should provide a secure and comfortable grip, be securely affixed to a full tang, and shouldn't get slippery when wet (wrapping the handle with friction tape or cloth tape might prove helpful). Avoid thin flimsy blades that flex, and poorly tempered brittle blades that can snap. Flimsy blades, like those of bread knives or filet knives, should only be used to slash with, as they will break or bend if stabbed into bone.

A sharp knife can either cut or stab. Cuts and slashes are best used to repel an assault, but can be deterred by heavy clothing—aim for the hands and face . Deep stabs to the torso can easily kill. Because a knife is a relatively small weapon, you must be close enough for your assailant to grab or strike you for it to be used effectively. Because of its short range, it often is not as menacing as one might hope—especially against violent criminals familiar with its weaknesses. Do not overextend yourself! Your moves must be quick, powerful, and precise. Unless you are determined and wary, you can easily be incapacitated or disarmed by a bold attacker. The simple knife is only effective against an armed assailant or multiple opponents in skilled hands. A highly skilled knifefighter can effectively wield two blades simultaneously, doubling his potential as a weapon. Only a master can throw a knife effectively in a combat situation, and even *he* is not guaranteed success (even at extremely close range)—*never throw your knife!*

A knife specialist will usually invest in a well made version of a design he is comfortable with, as not only do people favor knives with differing balance points and grips, but the various styles of knifefighting are best implemented with specific tools. For example, various styles favor the: Ka-Bar, stiletto, dirk, Bowie, *kukri,* or any of a variety of exotically curved blades. All the aforementioned knives have varying advantages and disadvantages, and are wielded via unique methods utilizing the strengths conferred to a particular design. Before purchasing a quality fighting knife, ascertain that it feels comfortable in your hand and is of a design compatible with your fighting style.

SWORDS:

A sword is an excellent choice, as it can legitimately be displayed on one's wall for decorative purposes even in jurisdictions where most weapons are prohibited. Most swords, however, are worthless for actual use because of shoddy construction. The vast majority of swords available are shoddy "wall-hangers" made of cheap alloys (such as zinc) that shatter when struck or will not take an edge. Even "stainless steel" versions often prove brittle and dull. Others are too unwieldy to actually use, or have handles that become loose after a few swings.

Most "samurai swords," *wushu* broadswords, scimitars, and decorative claymores are not worth your money. Many are dull edged atrocities (hammered out of an old truck bumper by some toothless foreigner in a loincloth), which are often given a cheap chrome plating that eventually peels off—you might be better served by an aluminum yardstick! Even the "stainless steel" fantasy swords you pay over a hundred dollars for tend to have weak "rat-tail" tangs and brass hardware, making them unsuitable for the rigors of demonstrations or staged swordfights—thus totally inappropriate for actual combat use. Very few companies, even the ones purporting to supply martial artists, offer quality swords usable as actual weapons. Museum Replicas Limited is the only company I can personally endorse as offering a wide selection of high quality weapons (designed for actual combat use as well as aesthetics) for a reasonable price. You can expect to spend at least $150 for a quality sword...and it will probably be well worth it.

In choosing a sword for home defense, you want one short enough (under 36" overall) to be swung effectively within a confined area. This will eliminate the claymore, longsword, and *tachi*. It should also be under three pounds, allowing it to be effectively wielded with one hand.

The Roman *gladius* (having a wide double-edge and a needle sharp point) is, by far, the best designed close combat sword ever designed, but prices typically start at around $275. However, a cheap and nasty alternative is available. The *qama* is a similarly styled weapon indigenous to Soviet Georgia. A passable replica is manufactured in India from high carbon steel and is available from Atlanta Cutlery for about $35. It is inferior to the *gladius*, but would certainly get the job done.

The Japanese *wakizashi* (having a keen edge of layered steel and an armor-piercing chisel- point tip) is a compact version of the *katana* designed specifically for fighting in corridors and alleyways, and is available from many sources from a starting price of around $70 for a stainless steel replica with riveted hardwood grips, to about $400 for a high-tech version from Cold Steel (the *Magnum Tanto XII*, with Kra-ton grip and a 12" blade of layered *San Mai* steel), to over $850 for a sword fashioned by classical methods from Bugei. Cold steel now imports top quality reproductions of classic Japanese and Chinese swords, and their classic *wakazashi* retails at $600.

The *Black Wind Katana* from Ontario Knife Company has a 20" blade made from 1070 carbon steel with black epoxy finish and a nylon paracord wrapped grip. Its overall length is just over 30". It costs about $100, but is a much better buy than the cheap imported "ninja swords" of similar appearance. The "Short Sword" from Junglee has a blackened AUS-8 stainless steel blade, rubberized grip, and an overall length exceeding 21"—it also costs about $100, and would be a fine choice.

If you want a sword, but cannot spend hundreds of dollars, military swords of decent quality can often be found at auctions, estate sales, and even garage sales. Most of the stuff sold at flea markets is cheap junk mass-produced overseas. Cavalry sabers, naval cutlasses, and dress uniform rapiers are all usually made from good quality steel that will take an edge and be functional for jabbing. Heavy military swords, like the cutlass, can chop almost as efficiently as a hatchet (the knees and wrists are quite vulnerable to such attacks). A rusted sword with loose grips can be had for as low as $10 and usually can be restored to ser-viceable condition within several hours. Better quality swords are usu-ally in the $50 - $200 price range (for collectibles as well as replicas). If you intend to display the sword prominently, and cost is not an issue, a functional antique sword in good condition could simply be tightened up and resharpened. As you won't likely be wearing it on your belt, a sheath is unnecessary. A wall mount can be purchased or fabricated at little expense, or it can be laid on the floor beneath your sofa or bed (just be sure keep it oiled, and wipe it down occasionally).

Bayonets, particularly the extra-long versions from the WWI era, are an effective substitute for a shortsword. They are extremely sturdy, but rarely take a keen edge. They are more like a pointed steel bar than a sword, and usually have small grips. They are only effective for jabbing, but could easily crack bones if swung hard. Used bayonets of acceptable quality can be had at prices between $20 and $75.

Regardless of what you might've seen in various action films and horror movies, machetes usually are not very effective. They seldom have a usable point, and often will not take a keen edge. Most machetes have wide blades fashioned from thin (1/8") metal, which decreases its mass. "Bowie" or "*tanto*" style blades (as well as sawbacks) may *look* scary, but fail to drastically improve performance. A "bolo" or "soft beak" design, however, will increase the force of your blows due to the additional weight near the tip. Machetes can only be used to chop with (with the notable exception of certain narrow bladed "*pangas*"), but are a frightful sight to behold, causing all but the most stouthearted to flee. New machetes typically run between $5 and $25.

Swords are good weapons because they are intimidating, nearly impossible to grab away from someone, and have a fairly long reach. You can keep someone at a distance without too much difficulty, and you have a reasonable expectancy of chasing them off by running at them swinging. They require minimal training to be effective against an unarmed assailant. However, they are designed to slice flesh and pierce organs, drawing a considerable amount of blood ("deluge" might be a more appropriate term) in so doing, which makes them inappropriate for many individuals to use effectively. In skilled hands, the sword can easily dispatch several attackers armed with inferior weapons. A well made sword, in expert hands, is a fearsome thing to behold.

BATTLE AXE:

The medieval battle axe with steel shaft and backspike is one of the most devastating primitive weapons one can be confronted with. It is designed to pierce armor, cleave skulls, and hack off limbs. A quality replica costs upwards of $100, and can legally be hung on one's wall. Most inexpensive replicas are composed of low quality alloy and assembled with epoxy, thus rendering them unusable as either tools or weapons.

A more commonly encountered alternative to the battle axe is the hatchet. A quality hatchet with steel shaft and rubberized grips (such as those made by Estwing) is far deadlier than any mere knife or club. The cheaper camp hatchets with hardwood handles are effective, but inferior. More than once, I've seen the head of such a hatchet come loose, either sliding down the shaft or flying off. Military "rescue axes" are also a good choice. Replicas of medieval hand axes often prove to be viable weapons. Most tomahawks, however, are too lightweight to inflict heavy damage, but their lack of mass enables them to be used with far more deftness. Taylor cutlery makes a reproduction of the *Vietnam Combat Tomahawk* (which features a sharpened backspike) for about $20. Some drywall hammers appear similar to an artist's conception of a futuristic tomahawk, and tend to be both sturdier and deadlier due to their superior construction.

A quality hatchet will kill or disable with a single blow. However, due to the weight of the head, it is difficult to redirect a missed swing and seconds are wasted between swings, leaving you vulnerable to attack. Furthermore, a missed downward swing can result in a self inflicted wound to the shinbone. Full sized axes are much too cumbersome for fighting with.

The heavy cleaver and meat ax are similar weapons, but tend to be thinner and lighter with far less reach—thus capable of less damaging blows. A properly modified spade can serve similarly in hacking at one's enemies. The infantryman's hand spade was sharpened on all three sides by the Soviet SPETsNAZ (often spelled: *spetsnaz*) and used both to chop with and to throw. A quality reproduction of the *spetsnaz* hand spade is available from Cold Steel for about $18, and Soviet surplus hand spades in good used condition can be had from various sources for under $10.

The axe murderer is an archetype. He dwells in the subconscious mind along with the hook-handed psychopath and the monster under the bed. 95% of all people confronted with someone charging them while swinging a hatchet and screaming will shit their pants (metaphorically or otherwise). To an unarmed man, it is like facing a chainsaw or sawed-off shotgun. It is one of the most psychologically devastating weapons you can employ.

SPEAR:

Spears come in a wide variety of configurations, from the thinly tapered javelin to the awkward jousting lance. For our purposes, we want one which is both compact (eliminating most polearms, harpoons, the Japanese *yari* and *naganta*, and the war lances of the Plains Indians), and effective (eliminating frogging forks and javelins designed for athletic competition).

The finest close combat spear ever invented is the Zulu *assegai*, with a short shaft and a long, wide, double-edged blade that can both jab and cut. Cold Steel offers an excellent version for about $45. The Cold Steel *assegai* is so well made you can literally use it to chop down a small tree.

Most boar spears and leaf-head spears are good, but the shaft must be cut down to a length between three and four feet for indoor use. Most Chinese *wushu*-style spears are too flimsy to be used for actual fighting, with unsharpened alloy heads attached to shafts with epoxy or tacks.

A cheap and nasty spearlike weapon is the *Mega Night Watchman* from United Cutlery. It consists of a 22.5" metal nightstick that unscrews to reveal a low quality 12" blade which can be threaded onto the shaft, forming a spear with an overall length of about 34". This device would be illegal in jurisdictions where nightsticks or sword canes are prohibited, but the law could be circumvented by epoxying it permanently in the spear configuration—this would also prevent the head from loosening up (and possibly detaching) while being used, which would be most embarrassing. I have seen versions of this crudely fashioned weapon, being sold via mail-order, in the $10 to $20 price range.

A make-shift spear can be fabricated from a kitchen knife and a length of broomstick or steel tubing, but is only as reliable as the strength of their connection. Screws, wire, epoxy, and duct tape can all be utilized, but such an improvised weapon will always be inferior to a weapon designed to withstand the rigors of combat. Most improvised spears tend to separate after several jabs at a practice target. Faux spearheads, such as are sometimes encountered atop decorative flagpoles, are generally hollow castings with rounded tips and thus inadequate for use as weapons.

Spears are used primarily for jabbing and clubbing, and never should be thrown. They are best employed with both hands grasping the shaft spaced at least a foot apart, using quick jabs and powerful thrusts. The shaft can be swung around to club or block with, but that would be inappropriate in most combat situations. If the shaft is grasped by a significantly larger or stronger assailant, your weapon can easily be immobilized or wrenched away.

CLUBS:

The club was primitive man's first tool. Virtually anything can be picked up and used as an improvised bludgeon with which to bop your fellow primates upon the noggin. Any stick, rod, or shaft between the lengths of one and four feet and weighing under five pounds will make a functional club. Clubs are better than blades for most people, because they are less likely to shed blood or kill—an individual who would be reluctant to defend himself with a kitchen knife often will not hesitate to pick up a broomstick with which to strike an attacker. The presence or addition of projections on the striking surface will transform a club into a mace, but such a modification can make it an illegal weapon. Billy clubs, nightsticks, and extendable batons are illegal in many jurisdictions, but a stout cane or length of broomstick is legal to possess anywhere.

Probably your best choice of club is the socially acceptable multi-celled aluminum flashlight. The police favor clubbed flashlights (popular brands include: Mag-Lite, Streamlight, and Kel-Lite) which hold 5 or 6 D-cell batteries, are incredibly bright, and can be run over by a tractor trailer without breaking. These lights come in various styles, including colored, rechargeable, and miniature versions. The flashlights can hold between 2 and 8 batteries, and have a beam that adjusts from spot to flood. The C-cell versions are best for speed and secure grip. Maximum strength batteries are noticeably heavier than standard cells, but are unnecessary. Aluminum flashlights can legally be carried in one's vehicle or on one's person in nearly every jurisdiction. These flashlights can easily crack bones, and a blow to the head can be fatal. A 6-cell aluminum flashlight will cost about $25.

Baseball bats are usually too awkward to swing inside a room or hallway. A much better choice would be the lightweight aluminum "tee-ball" bat used by small children to hit a stationary ball before they're ready for actual pitches. These bats weigh about a pound and are just over two feet in length. They can be had with rubberized grips, and a skilled stickfighter can effectively wield two such bats simultaneously. They are incredibly quick, compact, easily swung with one hand, and can be used effectively by someone with no weapons training. Tee-ball bats start at about $15.

"Rebar" is the name commonly given to the thin, knurled steel reinforcing rod used for strengthening concrete constructions. A small piece of rebar, from two to four feet in length, is much heavier than it looks. The grip must be wrapped with tape, as the surface is rough and often rusty. Rebar is one of the most devastating bludgeons known to man, as it will destroy virtually anything it comes into contact with, and is nearly indestructible. A length of rebar can easily smash through a wooden door or shatter cinderblocks—It is the poor man's "lightsaber." Rebar is freely available from construction sites and junkyards.

Hardwood dowels and lengths of steel pipe make effective clubs, and can be had for free in most attics, basements, and garages. A length of broomstick can easily be cut to any size and sanded smooth. Rattan *escrima* sticks can be purchased from martial arts suppliers, and various types of billy club, side-handle batons, and telescopic batons can be acquired, but are classified as illegal weapons in many jurisdictions.

Hammers make fine light maces. The ballpeen hammer is a favorite weapon of outlaw bikers, and comes in a variety of weights and lengths. Ballpeen hammers can easily be slipped into a back pocket, and are wicked in a fight. Light mallets generate a lot of power, but often are too heavy to use quickly. The framing hammer has a metal shaft, rubberized grip, and a straightened nail-extracting claw which makes a functional backspike.

Fireplace pokers often make good maces, but many are made of soft metal or have uncomfortable grips which can come loose. A top quality poker is better than a length of rebar, and its presence in your home is justifiable provided you have a fireplace or woodburning stove.

Maces can be fabricated from broomsticks cut to size and studded with nails. It is unnecessary for the points to be exposed, as the nail heads are just as effective. Screws or tacks can also be used. I once saw a wooden baseball bat with eight large carriage bolts set into the end, but it was ridiculously heavy. All such fabricated maces are usually considered to be illegal weapons. For about a hundred dollars, a top quality replica of a medieval mace can be purchased from Museum Replicas Limited. Replica maces are available in a variety of styles, from stone age warclubs to ornate scepters, many of which could easily serve as a socially acceptable display piece.

Short metal bars, axe handles, pool cues, jack handles, crowbars, lug wrenches, crescent wrenches, monkey wrenches, large candlesticks, table legs, various gardening tools, and certain sporting goods can all be used as improvised weapons in an emergency, but each has significant disadvantages and should not be selected as your primary weapon. For example, golf clubs and croquette mallets are usually too flimsy to rely upon for a second strike, and heavy cudgels often prove to be awkward weapons which make recovery from a missed swing difficult (if not impossible).

Clubs can be easily used by anyone, but their primary disadvantage is their low intimidation value. People just do not respect a club as much as a sharp blade. If you are facing a group, or a significantly larger assailant, you can reasonably expect your attacker(s) to boldly charge you and attempt to wrestle your weapon away in order to beat and sodomize you with it. Due to this fact, you must aggressively launch a pre-emptive strike, viciously and repeatedly striking your attacker until he retreats or is incapacitated (the shins, kness, and fore-arms make excellent targets). A club is a poor threat.

SCOURGES:

Scourges (commonly referred to as "whips") encompass a variety of non-lethal weapons including true whips (such as the bullwhip) as well as flexible rods and light chains. Scourges can be used to injure an enemy from a distance, can be used to engage multiple opponents, and tend to be used with even less hesitation than a club due to their low risk of inflicting serious injury; but most cannot be used effectively at close range, and longer whips would be awkward to use indoors.

In my opinion, the finest whiplike weapon available is the *sjambok*. *Sjamboks* are indigenous to South Africa and were originally fashioned from rhinoceros hide (which could easily split skin) and used for crowd control. Today, they are made from a stiff length of flexible plastic with a handle attached; they come in several lengths (36", 41", or 54"), and are available from Cold Steel for under $10 (the ribbed plastic grip it comes with can bite uncomfortably into uncallused hands, so it should either be smeared with epoxy and slipped into a bicycle handgrip, or cut away entirely with a thick wrapping of friction tape being used instead). The *sjambok* is swung like a rod and leaves incredibly painful welts which will repel nearly any assailant. When swung full force, it can even split clothing and inflict lacerations. It is incredibly fast, very effective, and can be used by an unskilled individual to repel a small group. Due to its extremely light weight, one can change direction, feint, and launch multiple combination attacks with lightning speed. It can only be countered by severance with a large sharp knife. It is impossible to kill with the plastic *sjambok* unless your target goes into shock from a relentless beating and is denied medical attention. It is a safe and efficient weapon that even many pacifists could be compelled to use under proper circumstances. Although not specifically prohibited, since it is specifically designed for use as a weapon it may be unlawful to possess in certain jurisdictions.

Another flexible rod is the *lathi*, which is also available from Cold Steel. The *lathi* is a rattan staff, between 3 and 6 feet in length, used in India (as well as the tropics) for crowd control as well as "caning" (a form of public corporeal punishment). Due to the pliant nature of the rattan fiber, these rods are unlikely to break bones, although the possibility exists. Even though the *lathi* is relatively lightweight for a wooden staff, it can still inflict a concussion or rupture internal organs if wielded too enthusiastically. Due to its rigidity, it can also be used to jab with.

Some automobile radio antennas can make a fine improvised whip. They will leave nasty welts, and can even split the skin. If the tip is sharpened, they can be used to jab with like a flimsy rapier (which will immediately bend in the event that contact is made with bone). Collapsible antennas can sometimes be concealed in a pocket and snapped open when needed, but they are far inferior to the more substantial solid antennas. The antenna will do more damage dependant upon diameter; hence the thick antennas found upon older vehicles will cause greater injuries than the thin "whip" antennas used for some CB radios.

Yardsticks made from wood or aluminum can crack bone if contact is made with the edge, but will simply leave a stinging welt if the opponent is slapped with the flat side (although it may well break or bend). If a wooden yardstick is snapped, the sharp point can be driven into the throat or belly like a stake into sod.

A "switch" fashioned from a thin flexible branch of sturdy green wood, such as hickory, makes an effective lash that can inflict painful welts with lightning speed; but it is fragile and its appearance would not command respect from an adversary. Such a length of wood is generally considered legal to possess, and would be overlooked as a harmless piece of rubbish in most searches.

Fishing poles made from bamboo, fiberglass, or graphite can be used to inflict stinging welts, and a multi-pronged hook at the end can cause painful lacerations (or bind in clothing), but they tend to be poor weapons that break easily and fail to inspire respect.

Chains can be considered either whips or flails, dependant upon weight. Light chains with small links (such as dog leads) can be used to whip an opponent mercilessly with little fear of breaking bones or inadvertently killing him (although flesh could be torn, resulting in maiming). An impressive concealable version of the light chain can be seen in the movie *Dragon* (based loosely upon the life of Bruce Lee), and consisted of approximately 3 feet of round link chain (to eliminate the possibility of links locking together) affixed to a small wooden handle by a swivel—such a weapon can be used to whip, trap, throw, choke, and bind. Medium weight chains, between 3 and 5 feet in length, can be used to effectively keep several opponents at bay, can easily break bones if contact is made, and can kill if the head, throat, or neck is struck with force. A medium weight chain is similar to a multi-segmented length of rebar in its lethal effectiveness, but with less destructive capability. Heavy chains and chains with weighted ends are considered flails.

True whips fall into several distinct categories: decorative and functional. Decorative whips are found far more often than usable ones, and include souvenirs, wall hangers, and sex toys; they are not intended for use as weapons, are generally of shoddy construction, and will do little more than sting an adversary, even if struck in the face. Functional whips include riding crops, "cats," and bullwhips.

A properly made riding crop is typically about 3 feet in length and consists of leather wrapped around a flexible rod and topped with a small slapper. Riding crops are capable of leaving nasty welts, splitting open exposed flesh, or taking out an eye, but they are only effective at close range and will not repel a determined attacker.

"Cats" are typically short multi-tailed whips (between 3 and 9 "tails") with a single handle, originally designed as a torture device. The majority of the cats in circulation fall into the "decorative" category (usually having only individual strips of leather rather than properly braided tails). Those which are intended to inflict injury can be modified by soaking in brine or by affixing barbs (typically fish hooks) to the ends.

Bullwhips (and the less commonly encountered horsewhips) are very long whips of thickly braided leather with a flat "cracker" at the end; today, they are most commonly used in demonstrations of skill. Bullwhips are substantial weapons intended for outdoor use only, and although shorter versions can be had, they often have lengths exceeding 20 feet. A bullwhip requires extensive practice before it can be used effectively as a weapon, and then it can tear flesh, rout multiple aggressors, and even strike small targets with great accuracy. At close range, the weighted handle can be swung like a flail or used to hammer with.

FIGHTING PICK:

This is my personal favorite, and is one of the deadliest hand weapons known to man. It is, in effect, a blade (curved or straight) or spike set perpendicular to the end of a shaft, and has enormous potential for deep penetration.

Examples of fighting picks include medieval warhammers with long backspikes, the war adze, the Japanese *kama*, the Hindi and Persian crowbills, the spontoon tomahawk of the Plains Indians, the light halberd, types of warclub fashioned from trade knives, the mattock, the entrenching tool, the light pick, the sickle, the ice axe, the mason's hammer, the mountaineer's pick, large hooks, and the proverbial "board with a nail." Primitive fighting picks typically had wooden shafts with heads fashioned from the same piece of wood, stone, volcanic glass, bronze, jade, or animal tusk. The barbed picks once used by salt miners are especially wicked in appearance, although their design would inhibit extraction from an enemy.

The fighting pick is used to stab via a powerful clubbing motion, and does not slash or chop effectively. It is deadlier than a knife and quicker than a hatchet. Heavy clothing will not deter it, and most types will defeat soft body armor—medieval fighting picks were designed specifically to puncture plate mail. A pick will easily pierce the skull. It has the potential to cause massive injury with every blow.

This weapon is incredibly wicked looking and will intimidate even the hardest of opponents. A skilled practitioner whirling two picks or sickles in a high speed kata makes one think of what the Grim Reaper might look like after smoking PCP. This weapon is scary just hanging on the wall.

FLAIL:

This weapon is listed nearly last due to the high degree of skill needed to utilize it effectively without injuring oneself. The flail is a flexible weapon, and comes in many variations. Novice martial artists often injure themselves while practicing, so this is for advanced students only.

Examples of flail include the medieval flail (commonly referred to incorrectly as a "mace" or "ball and chain"), Okinawan *nunchaku* (sometimes called "numchucks" or "chukka sticks" by the illiterate), the Japanese *manrikikusari* (fighting chain), the *wushu* steel whip (usually comprised of 7 or 9 linked steel rods), Chinese meteor balls, weights and blades attached to long cords, the spring cosh, and improvised weighted chains.

The medieval flail is composed of a weight (sometimes bristling with spikes) attached to a chain (usually under a foot in length) which is fastened to a ring or swivel atop a long wooden handle (usually about two feet in length). It is usually designed so the weight can be swung freely without possibility of accidentally colliding with the weapon hand. It is an efficient and extremely deadly weapon, its only shortcoming being the swivel, which usually is not on a par with modern standards. Many inexpensive replicas are not functional as weapons.

The *nunchaku* is two rods (usually wood, but sometimes acrylic, aluminum, or even steel water pipe), usually either 12" or 14" in length, connected by a short cord or chain. Smaller versions (usually 8") are called "mini-chucks," and are only good for sapping people from behind. *Nunchaku* are usually made from rounded sticks, which are favored by most practitioners, but if they are to be used as weapons you should get octagonal or studded sticks to inflict maximum damage. This weapon has injured more novice practitioners than all others combined and tripled—many *karateka* have ended up in emergency rooms after fracturing their own skulls while trying to imitate Bruce Lee . If you are going to use these as a weapon, use only one set and don't try any slick moves—just hold one stick and wail at your opponent's head, shoulders, arms, and knees as hard and as fast as you can. The free-swinging stick flies blindingly fast, even in the hands of an amateur. It can be defended against, but it is nearly impossible to block. *Nunchaku* are illegal to carry concealed nearly everywhere, but in many (not all) jurisdictions you can possess them in your residence, especially if you have official certification from a recognized martial arts academy and no criminal history. In some misguided jurisdictions, owning two pieces of sawed-off broomstick connected together with a shoelace carries a stiffer sentence than carrying a concealed unlicensed handgun.

The *manrikikusari* is a pair of metal weights connected by a length of chain (usually about two feet). The ones typically available from martial arts suppliers have cylindrical metal handles about 6" long. A similar weapon, the *kusari-fundo*, typically has multi-faceted ball-like weights in lieu of handles. The fighting chain can be used to whup ass pretty good, but its primary strength lies in its ability to block, bind, and trap sword and stick attacks. Being flexible along its entire length, it is a difficult weapon to master and is best left to advanced students.

Meteor balls, conical weights, rope darts, rope knives, steel whips, the *shogue,* the *kusarikama,* and other long range flexible weapons (such as the bullwhip) are only useful in the hands of an expert. It would take several months of daily practice to gain even basic proficiency with these weapons, so they are best left alone. They are only suited to outdoor use anyway.

The spring cosh, unlike the non-lethal telescopic coil spring baton, is a deadly weapon designed to crush skulls. It consists of a heavy weight on the end of a long stiff coil spring affixed to a grip. This weapon was designed for trench warfare during WWI and might be considered a "super-blackjack." While the blackjack is designed to subdue, the cosh is designed to kill. It is highly illegal, and I've never seen one offered for sale to the general public, though examples can be seen in museums and the weapon would be simple to duplicate. If you are found in possession of a spring cosh, unless it is a valuable antique locked in an inaccessible display case, you are going to prison.

Flails can be improvised by affixing a padlock to a short length of chain, putting a rock or battery in a sock or stocking, tying a light weight (such as a fishing sinker) to a length of cord, or freeing one's heavily buckled belt. If nothing of sufficient mass is available, you can use a bar of soap, a handful of sand, a pocketful of change, half a bag of hard candies, or a small hardcover book to weight your sock, bandanna, or pillowcase. In an emergency, even a small appliance firmly attached to a power cord can be used.

The belt is a fine improvised flail. It is commonly wrapped once or twice around one's hand and swung in a "figure-8" motion. Thin belts with light buckles can be used to whip and trap. Thick belts with heavy buckles can be used to break bones, crack skulls, and even kill. All serious students of self-defense need to familiarize themselves with the basics of beltfighting—it is a legal and everpresent improvised weapon that can easily thwart a knife attack.

A flail is much quicker and generates far more power than a rigid club, is nearly impossible to block or grab, and is an intimidating sight in skilled hands. However, it should not be chosen unless you're willing to devote countless practice hours developing mastery of it. If you have not practiced enough to familiarize yourself with this weapon and learn its limitations, you will probably injure yourself. Flexible weapons usually are inefficient and counter-productive in the hands of a novice.

MISSILE WEAPONS:

Missiles have been left until last, because they require even more practice and skill than the treacherous flexible weapons. You need to practice hitting targets regularly, or will eventually lose the ability to do so. Missiles allow you to engage targets at far greater ranges than other primitive weapons, but often prove unsatisfactory for extremely close contact—in the event that you are rushed, it is good to have a backup weapon (such as a hammer or butcher knife) to rely upon.

Most missile weapons are too clumsy, inefficient, or impractical to seriously consider for protection. These include, but are by no means limited to: throwing knives, throwing stars (*shaken*), throwing spikes (*shuriken*), large ball bearings, darts, lawn jarts, javelins, boomerangs, blowguns, longbows, spearguns, and slings. A few of the better choices of primitive missile weaponry will be examined.

A crossbow is intimidating, but only allows for a single shot unless you have a full minute to reload (crossbow pistols are nearly worthless). A compound bow, in the hands of an expert, can be fired accurately every five seconds until arrows are depleted. The head, throat, chest, and midsection are all viable targets. Fired from a crossbow or compound bow, a quality chisel-tipped broadhead will easily penetrate bone, possibly passing completely through one's target. Arrows will kill, but have little stopping power, so unless the brain or heart is struck, an attack may continue until the target bleeds out or shock sets in.

Blackpowder revolvers in .44 caliber are legal to purchase without restriction in many jurisdictions—even via mailorder—and are about as powerful as a .38 special. They give you five or six shots as well as produce a disorienting and acrid smokescreen. Kept dry, they are reliable and effective, but a certain degree of skill and knowledge is required to load them and many will discharge if dropped in such a way that the hammer strikes the floor. Muzzleloading pistols give you only one shot, and tiny hideout guns (like the .31 caliber snake-eyes derringer) have less stopping power than the woefully inadequate .25 ACP.

Wristbrace slingshots, which are illegal in many jurisdictions, can kill if steel ball bearings are fired at the head or throat. They can be fired rapidly and accurately with great power. Slingshots lacking a wristbrace are low-powered and nearly worthless.

Throwing stars are typically garbage. Even the good ones don't work that well. Heavy 4 or 5 pointed stars made from thick tool steel and highly sharpened can be effective, provided you have at least a half-dozen. Effective *shaken* are at least six inches in diameter and weigh over a pound—such a weapon can easily kill. The head and throat are viable targets, but the torso and arms can be struck as well.

Steel ball bearings and solid meditation balls are legal to own, are capable of cracking bones, and can be thrown with far greater accuracy than a rock or billiard ball. They can easily be dropped in one's pockets without worrying about the possibility of snagging upon withdrawal, but are difficult to conceal. These weapons will leave painful lumps anywhere they strike, and can even cause a concussion if the cranium is impacted, but you'll need about a dozen carried in a pouch if you are seriously considering them as a primary weapon. The pouch itself would then become a lethal flail, and individual balls could make devastating fistloads.

Heavy washers (2 grade, #1 washers, approx. 5 to a pound) work great as missile weapons, although their damage potential is rather limited. However, due to their availability, flat profile, legality, and low price (you could pick up two dozen for the cost of a single flea market throwing star), they are highly recommended. With practice, they can be thrown forcefully and accurately a variety of ways (overhand, backhand, or underhand), and by grasping them through the center hole, a cluster of three can be thrown simultaneously for a "scattergun" effect. Although it would be nearly impossible to actually kill someone with these things, the "hurtful disks of pain" can be used to drive off light-weight threats or disconcert a serious threat, enabling you to escape. One can easily conceal a half- dozen disks on one's person, and affixing a lanyard (paracord, fishing line, twine, or a bootlace) to one will transform it into a light flail.

Much nastier than silly wafer-like throwing stars are circular saw blades. These come in various styles, and can range from cheap to expensive, but must be thrown so they spin in the proper direction to be effective. It is terrifying to have circular saw blades thrown at you with force, and the majority of assailants would immediately vacate the area upon seeing you brandish a handful. As it is possible to snag and tear the flesh between your thumb and forefinger while throwing (even during practice), it is advised that you wear a tight-fitting unlined leather glove (preferably fingerless) for a bit of protection. Next to the Cold Steel *Torpedo* (a double-pointed *shuriken* throwing spike 15" long and weighing 2 lbs), circular saw blades are probably the most devastating thrown weapon known to man (yes, I've considered the *hunga-*

munga, hurlbat, *chakrum*, and Irish dart)—and they can be purchased in bulk at the hardware section of any department store. A half dozen or more can be kept in a thin leather satchel with shoulder strap for quick access and ease of transport. If you feel compelled to practice throwing circular saw blades, please practice only on dead trees, fence-posts, and wooden crates with a proper backstop—and be prepared to hop out of the way if one bounces back at you (wrapping your target with several layers of cardboard will reduce the likelihood of a rebound).

"Choose Your Weapons!"

Someday, you may find yourself in a situation where you will be required to protect yourself, or other people (possibly: family, friends, neighbors, or co-workers, any of whom you might feel responsible for the safety of, dependant upon circumstances), from a vicious animal, a deranged individual, or a group of predatory criminals intent on inflicting grievous physical harm. In such dire circumstances, there is a very high risk that you could be seriously injured or even killed.

Be advised—you can incur substantial penalties for "taking the law into your own hands," so engaging in combat should be avoided through whatever alternatives are available to you (flight, negotiation, calling 911, etc.), especially if you find yourself compelled to defend another person without benefit of all the facts—after all, the very person you perceive as an innocent victim might very well have provoked the unlawful attack through past misdeeds!

By picking up a weapon, you face a substantial risk of injury or incarceration—think about the probable result of your actions. If you might, in effect, be "throwing your life away" by the act of engaging the perceived threat, you must ask yourself if it is really worth it. Is there no other alternative? Would you be content if this were your last act on Earth? Sometimes a warrior must interpose himself between a threat and the people that he loves, but the majority of fights are initiated by far lesser things, like the simple exchange of offensive words. If you are one of those clowns who is willing to kill or die over an insult, be aware that in the eyes of the law, the media, and society at large, you will be judged to be insecure, dangerous, and wrong. *"If you must fight, make sure that you're right."*

In such a scenario, you will need to arm yourself to increase your probability of success. In many situations, you may be forewarned of impending danger. You may have several minutes—or only a few seconds—in which to secure the best possible tool for the task at hand. If you have taken prior precautions and have a suitable weapon on your person or in the immediate vicinity, this will not present a dilemma. Take a few moments and inspect your surroundings…what nearby items could you use as an improvised weapon? After weighing your options, you will quickly see that not all weapons are created equal—some might prove horrendously effective, while others might only serve as a minor irritant. It is always a good idea to scan your environment for possible weapons that you could use in an emergency—or that others could pick up and use against *you*.

In this section, I have compiled a list of weapons one could use to defend themselves. The weapons are graded based on their perceived effectiveness (although opinions vary and each situation is different) with a letter-grade of "A" through "F." Furthermore, each letter-graded category is titled, and the weapons therein are listed in order of precedence. In some instances, additional comments have been added for clarification. This listing is meant to be a concise introduction to the subject of weapon selection, so numerous omissions may be noted.

A
FIREARMS

If a firearm and ammunition are available to you, it should be your primary choice in nearly all defensive scenarios. Combining power, range, and intimidation, most modern firearms are devastatingly effective versus unarmored opposition—even in relatively unpracticed hands. The opinions expressed about the comparative "stopping power" of various cartridges are based on several factors and considered reasonably accurate, but you may feel free to dispute them if you wish.

1.   AUTO RIFLE: A modern autoloading rifle (chambered for either .308 or .223), along with multiple high-capacity magazines and webgear, is the deadliest weapon available to the civilian populace (this category also includes the AR-15 style "pistols" with detachable magazines). Equipped with combat sights (holographic, red dot, or laser designator) it can accurately be fired at numerous moving targets anywhere from close to medium range. Compact scopes are more of a detriment than an asset unless you are engaging targets at long range. Chamberings in 7.62 X 39 Soviet and .30 Carbine are ballistically inferior and should be avoided. Needless to say, if overpenetration is a factor (as it would be in densely populated settings) this weapon should not be an option unless loaded with extremely expensive prefragmented projectiles (often over $5 per round!).

2.   COMBAT SHOTGUN: An automatic or pump shotgun with short (18"—22") barrel and bandoleer sling should be your primary weapon for home defense. Even when loaded with birdshot, a single shotgun blast to the center of mass is virtually guaranteed to instantly disable any unarmored target. 10 and 12 gauge shotguns are often recommended, but a 16 or 20 gauge is more than adequate for indoor use. The light 28 gauge can effectively be used by a frail person at point blank range, but the stopping power of the ultralight .410 gauge cannot be relied upon. A mounted high-intensity light greatly increases this weapon's effectiveness. Most experts recommend loading the defensive shotgun with either #1 or #00 buckshot, which I would generally agree with, but saboted slugs can also be used for long range accuracy and deep penetration. If you live in a populated area where overpenetration would be dangerous, it is recommended that you load your weapon either with #9 birdshot or non-lethal projectiles (like rubber buckshot or "beanbag" rounds).

3. COMBAT HANDGUN: A magnum revolver or military-style automatic is a viable alternative to the combat shotgun, though not nearly as powerful. Pistol caliber carbines (as well as the .30 M1 Carbine) and "assault pistols" (such as the TEC-9) would also fit into this category. Common calibers (in order of ascending lethality) include: 9mm, .40 S&W, .45ACP, .357 Sig, .357 magnum, .45 Long Colt, .41 magnum, and .44 magnum. Weapons in this category are best fitted with a laser designator or tactical light to increase accuracy.

4. DEFENSIVE HANDGUN: "Carry guns," such as snub-nosed revolvers and compact automatics of moderate power fall into this category. Common calibers (in order of ascending lethality) include: .38 special, .22 Winchester Magnum Rimfire, .380 ACP, .32 H&R magnum, and .44 special.

5. SPORTING FIREARMS: This category includes long-barreled break-action shotguns, bolt and lever action hunting rifles, high-powered single-shot handguns, black powder firearms, double-barreled "elephant guns," and .50 caliber "anti-material rifles." While most of these weapons are far more powerful than the average firearm and capable of incredible accuracy when fitted with proper optics, they tend to be cumbersome and have a slow rate of fire. These long-range weapons are difficult to use at close range, but far better than no gun at all.

6. PLINKERS: The lethal potential of the common .22 LR rimfire cartridge (especially high-velocity hollowpoints fired from a longer barrel) is widely underrated, although multiple shots to vital areas are often required to finish the job quickly. A .22 long arm or handgun can be found in one out of every four households. An autoloader with several high capacity magazines would be best—better, even, than most of the "sporting firearms."

7. HIDEOUT GUNS: Low-powered and inaccurate cub automatics, miniature revolvers, and derringers, as well as "novelty weapons" such as penguns. The most common chamberings (in order of ascending lethality) include: .41 rimfire, .32 short, .22 short, .25 ACP, .22 LR, .32 long, .32 ACP, and .22 WMR. With such impotent cartridges, one's best option is to either fire several rounds while running away or to close with one's enemy to press the muzzle against the stomach, throat, or ear for a contact shot—used in such a manner, these weapons have a little more stopping power than an automatic centerpunch. In many cases, a primitive weapon (such as a hatchet) might be a better choice. Some modern derringers will accept magnum and even rifle ammunition, which would greatly increase stopping power, but not accuracy.

8. FLAREGUNS: I know that signal flare projectors should not be included amongst the firearms, but no other category seemed to fit. A large flare pistol (or even a hand launched parachute flare) can seriously injure, or conceivably even kill, a person it is fired into from close range, although it is far more likely to either miss or rebound. Rubber inserts are available that allow one to fire the smaller 12 gauge flares which, with minor modifications, will also accept actual shotshells (although the resulting pressures could blow apart those orange plastic flareguns). 12 gauge "derringer-style" flareguns, miniature flare projectors, and "pen flares" are all nearly useless for self-defense, except to create a distraction. Flare-guns are extremely inaccurate (even at point-blank range) and present an extreme fire hazard when used indoors. A flaregun should not seriously be considered as a weapon unless no other option exists, although there's a lot to be said for the intimidation factor of staring down a 2" bore.

B
PRIMITIVE WEAPONS

Primitive weapons include reproductions of medieval armaments as well as classical martial arts weaponry. This category also includes similarly styled weapons, and certain weaponlike tools which can be practiced with as well as modified to increase their lethal potential.

1. SWORDS: Swords designed for actual combat use that are hefty, sturdy, and sharp, including broadswords, cutlasses, and *katanas*. A sword can easily keep several unarmed opponents at bay as it is nearly impossible to snatch it away from you.

2. SPEARS: Various iron and steel headed spears with short shafts—usually designed for hunting lions or wild boar. Best used for short quick jabs, although one can also club with the butt and block with the shaft. This is a good weapon, but a bold assailant could easily wrestle it away from you if provided with the opportunity to do so.

3. FLAILS: Quality reproductions of medieval ball-and-chain flails (few exist) as well as *nunchaku*. Devastating weapons, but often cause injury to inexperienced users.

4. PICKS: Various light picks and adzes, as well as war-hammers with long backspikes.

5. BATTLE-AXES: Medieval reproductions as well as steel-shafted hatchets.

6. SHORT SWORDS: Including machetes and long bayonets (c. WWI), which are both inferior to actual compact swords (like the gladius).

7. CLUBS: Including maces, warclubs, short aluminum bats, ax handles, and some hammers. Generally considered "less-than-lethal" provided the head is not struck.

8. SJAMBOKS: A flexible rod used primarily for crowd control—quick, effective, and non-lethal. Reproductions of this weapon are made using modern materials. This lightweight scourge can instinctively be wielded by anyone with excellent results.

9. LONG KNIVES: Substantial (full tang and thick steel) cutlery such as butcher, chef, and carving knives. Professional meatcutting knives often have blades over a foot long.

10. KNIVES: Sturdy fixed blade knives with blades under 8" long, including kitchen knives as well as hunting knives, tantos, and daggers.

11. WALLHANGERS: Low quality counterfeit swords that don't take an edge and rattle when shook. Such a decoration may intimidate an intruder, but will quickly fall apart during the rigors of actual use. This imported trash may be inexpensive, but it is worthless as a weapon and looks chintzy hanging on your wall...don't waste your money.

C
PERSONAL WEAPONS

Personal weapons are items—often overlooked as weapons—that one can carry on one's person while walking the streets. They are legal to possess nearly everywhere, do not present a threatening appearance to the general public, and are highly effective in the hands of a skilled martial artist (although they can readily be used by untrained persons as well).

1. PEPPERSPRAY: A highly effective non-lethal personal defense item that can be dropped in a pocket or purse. Used properly (which requires training), it will deter the majority of miscreants.

2. WALKING STICK: A stout cane or walking stick makes an effective quarterstaff, and a solid metal grip turns it into a lethal mace. Incredibly effective in the hands of an expert.

3. ALUMINUM FLASHLIGHT: A 2 or 3 cell flashlight does not appear nearly as menacing as the 6 cell illuminated nightsticks most cops favor (especially if a color other than black), and can be held in one's hand or slipped in a back pocket under one's jacket. It is capable of cracking bones wherever it strikes. For some reason, the D-cell versions are most popular, but the C-cell versions offer a far more secure grip. For added heft (if desired), maximum strength batteries may be used.

4. BELT: A leather belt with a solid metal buckle can be swung like a flail—it is incredibly quick and can do a surprising amount of damage. A lightweight dress or web belt can be used as a whip. The average belt will provide one with about yard of effective range, enabling one to keep a knife-wielding attacker at a distance.

5. LOCKBLADE: A quality folding knife with a locking blade is a weapon of last resort, but can inflict horrific wounds in the hands of a determined individual. Small knives are best employed against unarmed assailants—and only if no other weapon is available to you. Small knives are most useful in a grappling situation.

6. COMB: A steel or aluminum rattail comb can be used to rake, gouge, and stab an opponent with telling results—especially if the point has been sharpened. Combs and hairbrushes are available that conceal synthetic blades or spring-loaded spikes, but these are typically poor quality weapons as well as usually being illegal to possess.

7. KEYS: To use one's keys effectively as a weapon, they should be attached to a neck cord, chain, lanyard, or long tasseled fob in order to create an improvised flail, which can be swung with great force at the head and face of an attacker. Effectiveness will increase depending upon the length of the flexible section and the weight of the keyring.

8. YAWARA: A *kubotan* keychain attachment or aluminum penlight with weighted endcap can be used by a highly trained individual to attack various pressure points and nerve clusters. They are primarily intended for persons who wish to restrain someone without inflicting injury. In the hands of an unskilled person they can be used to augment hammerfist blows. They are a little better than nothing at all.

D
IMPROVISED WEAPONS

Improvised weapons found in this category are common objects which have great potential for defensive use; however, they have various faults which would discourage one from relying upon them as a primary weapon. Because they might be somewhat awkward to use, it is unlikely that one would gain familiarity with these objects through extensive practice; nonetheless, using one of these items would be far superior to launching an empty-handed attack.

1. BLUDGEONS: Primarily heavy tools with secure grips, such as wrenches and mallets, but would also include fireplace pokers, rolling pins, iron skillets, and suitable pieces of scrap metal. These are natural weapons which require no skill to use.

2. POLEARMS: Lightweight metal heads affixed to long wooden handles—primarily gardening tools such as hoes, rakes, and chop-

pers (although gaff hooks, frogging forks, and dual-tined pitch-forks also fall into this category). These tools provide one with great range and are intimidating when wielded competently. They may be used to jab or club with, but are best employed as quarter-staves.

3. SPORTING GOODS: Examples would include: baseball bats, golf clubs, ski poles, oars, pool cues, tennis rackets, lacrosse sticks, and croquette mallets, some of which might prove to be a poor choice of weapon due to flimsiness or other factors. If you use one of these items frequently, familiarity is attained to such a degree that it becomes like an extension of your body. Due to the many differences in form and function of the items in this category, they vary greatly in effectiveness as well as method of implementation.

4. PROBES: Screwdrivers, awls, and icepicks all combine a sharp-ened metal rod with a comfortable grip, and can be used effectively to puncture one's adversary; however, due to the lack of shock inflicted by this weapon, major blood vessels must be targeted if immediate results are desired. Because of this weapon's design, it is possible to penetrate the cranium or sternum with a forceful blow. Large hooks (stevedore or hay) would also be included in this cate-gory, but flimsy skewers would not.

5. POWER TOOLS: Few things are more fearsome than a Sawzall (or long-bar chainsaw), in the hands of an angry man (even drills and belt sanders can be used as deadly weapons—although to a lesser degree); however, such tools are cumbersome and may be limited to the range of an electrical cord (seldom more than 30 feet).

6. HEAVY TOOLS: Shovels, axes, crowbars, and similar items all can be used to inflict massive injuries; however, they are difficult to maneuver, easy to get around, and tire you out quickly.

7. SHARPS: Flimsy blades such as filet knives, bread knives, steak knives, linoleum knives, utility blades, craft knives, boxcutters, straight razors, and razor scrapers. Such blades can only be used to slash with, and repeated impacts can easily result in breakage. A short paring knife is usually a far better choice, due to its durability and capacity for penetration.

8. PROJECTILE WEAPONS: Most non-firearm projectile weapons are slow to reload and awkward to use at close range. This section was not included with the "Primitive Weapons" because the majority are of recent manufacture. I chose to include this section with the "Improvised Weapons" because many of these items are not designed as weapons and are ineffective when utilized as such.

    A compound bow or crossbow loaded with broadheads can injure or kill an attacker at moderate range, but arrows have little stopping power (unless the brain, throat, or heart is directly struck). A recurve or youth bow loaded with target arrows can kill if the throat or eye is struck, but is far more likely to do little more than enrage a determined attacker. A wrist-brace slingshot (which is illegal in some jurisdictions) can cause severe injuries if ball bearings or jagged rocks are fired.

    A high powered pellet rifle (such as the Sheridan 5mms) can kill if the eye or throat is struck, and has about the same stopping power as a .25 ACP pistol. Standard velocity BB and pellet guns have the capability to blind or maim if the face is repeatedly hit (as with a semi-automatic CO_2 pistol). Paintball guns can deliver painful welts as well as rupture an unprotected eye. Spearguns fire a single inaccurate shot that can be potentially lethal at close range (the solar plexus being the most viable target).

    Slings require a great deal of practice to use effectively, and would be difficult to whirl indoors. Blowguns are mostly useless unless the darts are pre-treated with dangerous and unlawful substances.

Throwing stars, throwing spikes, and darts (as well as bolts from pistol crossbows) are all crappy weapons that are best used to slow down pursuers. Most projectile weapons are valued more for their intimidation factor (due to their ability to inflict injury from a distance) than for their actual effectiveness.

9. BULLWHIPS: Bullwhips are difficult (if not impossible) to use indoors, and require extensive practice to be effective outdoors. They are not recommended for defensive use unless one is highly skilled in their use. At close range, the weighted handle can be swung like a flail. Be aware that the majority of whips on the market are low quality novelties intended for decorative use only.

E
NO WEAPON

You may find yourself in a situation where you desperately need a weapon but nothing suitable is at hand—in such instances, one must be creative. Almost anything can be implemented as a weapon in a crisis, and even a poor weapon is generally preferable to no weapon at all.

1. "ROCK IN A SOCK": A stone, brick fragment, flashlight battery, handful of gravel, or even a bar of soap can transform a sock or stocking into a potentially lethal improvised blackjack. This weapon takes only seconds to assemble, is incredibly fast, and is highly effective. By knotting off the end, a more secure grip is provided.

2. IMPROVISED WHIPS: Yardsticks, car antennas, fishing poles, broken automobile belts, bungee cords, extension cords, lengths of hose or tubing, an unwound wire clotheshanger, or even a "switch" snapped off a suitable tree branch are all things that can inflict painful welts on anyone daring to come within range. These weap-

ons are non- lethal, but will repel all but the most determined of unarmed attackers; however, they require a certain amount of skill to use effectively.

3. IMPROVISED BLUDGEON: A candlestick, lamp, bottle, or large ashtray can be used to beat someone with, but such items tend to be uncomfortable to grasp and easily broken, so they are awkward to use. Table legs, boards, and various lengths of scrap wood can all be utilized, with varying degrees of effectiveness (dependent upon size, composition, and condition).

4. THROWN OBJECTS: Dishes, canned goods, rocks, brick fragments, billiard balls, bottles, tools, flashlight batteries, rolled coins (pennies in plastic shrink wrappers work best) and other common items can be hurled at one's adversary to inflict injury and deter pursuit. Thrown objects give you extra range and generally put the recipient on the defensive, but they seldom do significant damage and you'll eventually run out of things to throw. Remember that whatever you throw at an adversary can be thrown back at *you* (unless it shatters).

5. CUDGELS: A cudgel is defined here as an extremely heavy object that is difficult to swing but will do an incredible amount of damage if it connects. Examples would include: sledgehammers, wood-splitting mauls, mop wringers, and bumper jacks. These weapons require both hands to swing and leave you vulnerable in the event you miss your target.

6. HOT STUFF: Nobody wants to be disfigured, so the threat of being burned is very effective. Hot things that most sane individuals would back away from include: irons, soldering irons, blowtorches (variations include torches using butane, propane, or acetylene, although torches utilizing other fuel sources may also be encountered), highway flares, red hot pokers, heated skillets, heated coffeepots, boiling water, burning liquids (such as flaming

beverages or melting shoe polish), corrosive chemicals (like sulfuric acid or drain cleaner), improvised torches (fabricated by wrapping a stick in fuel-soaked rags or dipping it in molten fuel), and automobile cigarette lighters (which often cool down within seconds)). Even though the aforementioned items are intimidating when brandished, they seldom cause serious injury (aside from possible scarring, which is usually cosmetic rather than incapacitating) capable of stopping a motivated attacker, and may present a serious fire hazard as well.

7.   NASTY SPRAYS: Include oven cleaner, pesticide, and spray paint. Unless you have a can of wasp & hornet killer, you probably only have an effective range of about three feet. These things can easily cause permanent blindness in addition to other ailments. Aerosol disinfectants are not quite as harmful, but can potentially cause serious injury to the eyes. Deodorant, hairspray, and foot spray can prove irritating as well as distracting, but are unlikely to inflict lasting damage. When grappling, the base of the can may be used as a bludgeon, but if your enraged assailant gets his hands on it you can be sure he'll attempt to spray *you* with it. Sprays are best used just prior to fleeing.

8.   ELECTRIC CURRENT: If you were to jab someone with the lit lightbulb of a household lamp, they would be jolted with 110 volts as the glass shattered and they contacted the filament (although such a weapon can only be used once). If the female end of an extension cord were to be cut off and the exposed wires stripped of insulation, it could be plugged into a wall outlet and snapped towards one's assailant—to make it even more effective, it could be lashed or taped to a broomstick and used as a prod. Attaching bare wires to a doorknob or damp carpet as a "boobytrap" only works reliably in the movies, and is *not* a viable option.

This suggestion is included for informational purposes only (although it has been irresponsibly mentioned in several other books), due to the fact that using electricity as a weapon is most ill advised, as the risks involved are significant. First, it would be extremely dangerous to handle live wires without insulated boots and gloves. Next, the physical effects of contact with household current are difficult to predict—a shock could result in burns, unconsciousness, death, or no discernable effect at all. And last, upon discharging household current into a human body, it is likely that a circuit breaker could trip, and it is even possible that the wiring could overheat—resulting in fire.

9. ANY POSSIBLE OBJECT: A small fraction of the possibilities include: broom, mop handle, the dowel from a windowshade, trash can lid, tape measure, briefcase, lunchbox, purse, coffee cup, stapler ,scissors, letter opener, telephone receiver, chair, clock, picture frame, toilet tank lid, toothpaste tube, pencil, pen, fork, hairbrush, paperweight, napkin dispenser, skewers, helmet, vase, knitting needles, potted plant, child's toy, drumsticks, dumbbells, a package of frozen meat, or pieces of broken glass. Anything solid, pointed, or sharp can be used as a weapon by a determined individual (with varying levels of effectiveness based upon skill, viciousness, and the object's suitability for the task).

10. A HANDFUL OF DUST: Sand, gravel, dirt, ashes, pencil shavings, scouring powder, pepper, salt, sugar, flour, spices, coffee, rice, dried beans, soup mix, salted peanuts, small candies, loose coins, or any handful of small objects can be thrown into an adversary's face to momentarily distract him, giving you opportunity to either attack an unprotected vital area or flee.

11. ENVIRONMENT: Forcing an opponent into contact with various features of your environment could prove extremely effective under the right circumstances. In addition to being pushed off a

roof or thrown out a window, your enemy could be forcefully introduced to the following hazards: cement floors, brick walls, open holes, fire hydrants, curbs, dumpsters, corners of buildings, plate glass, stairs, traffic, slamming doors, and dangerous machinery. Being slammed into any of these things will prove far more damaging than a simple punch or kick.

12. NOTHING: Kick, bite, and gouge—being unarmed makes you vulnerable, so it is imperative that you fight as viciously as possible in order to survive. For hand techniques, stick to hammerfists, palm heels, and elbow strikes—a punch to your opponent's head can easily result in broken fingers or a sprained wrist.

F
WORSE THAN NOTHING

Believe it or not, a few things are actually *worse than nothing!* A worthless item that gives one a false sense of confidence puts you at substantial risk. Many people would actually freeze upon being confronted with a rapidly unfolding crisis scenario and discovering that the one thing they were relying upon to protect them had *failed.* Do not give any of these bogus "defensive measures" a second thought.

1. STUNGUN: These silly toys consistently fail to perform as advertised. They are only useful for torturing helpless victims, which makes them worthless to everyone but sadists. They are only effective when forcibly held against sensitive areas for 10 seconds or longer, which is nearly impossible to achieve versus a physically superior assailant. Tasers and stun batons are a little more effective, but not much.

2. DEFECTIVE PEPPERSPRAY: Pepperspray (as well as teargas) canisters are offered by dozens of manufacturers—unfortunately,

many of them prove to be of poor quality. Poor quality pepper-spray dispensers may fail to function due to jammed buttons, internal misalignments, or other manufacturing defects. Furthermore, canisters could be empty, depressurized, or filled with a weak solution. Be certain that you buy only top quality products, keep the nozzle free of debris (like pocket lint), and discard after the expiration date—don't trust your life to some imported pepperspray that you found on sale at a convenience store.

3. HOME FABRICATED SPRAY WEAPONS: Some people advocate putting tabasco sauce, onion juice, or formaldehyde in water pistols and nasal spray dispensers to defend oneself with...please do not do this. Such "weapons" are utterly unreliable. They leak, have an extremely limited range, and deliver an inadequate amount of agent.

4. FAKE GUNS: Some imbeciles actually carry starter pistols, "stage guns," "counterfeit guns," inoperable guns, or even realistic looking toys in hopes of "frightening" a potential mugger or rapist. It is dangerous to bluff when your life is at stake, especially when a bold assailant might be tempted to wrest it away from you, knowing many people have a tendency to hesitate or "freeze up" upon realizing they might actually shoot someone. If an assailant discovers he's been threatened with a harmless prop, it is likely he'll become enraged and beat you severely. Furthermore, possession of fake guns is unlawful in many jurisdictions.

5. HATPINS: A sturdy hatpin *can* inflict serious injuries if precisely stabbed deep into vital areas; however, wounds caused by such a weapon will not effect an assailant's ability to fight until much later...perhaps hours later. Being stabbed with a hatpin will only serve to enrage an attacker, and they tend to bend or break quite easily. This flimsy "weapon" (as well as similar objects) has imbued many novices with a false sense of confidence.

6. KEYS PROTRUDING FROM FIST: Many self-defense manuals advocate grasping one's keys in the fist so that they protrude from between the fingers in a clawlike fashion. In theory, this appears to be a good idea; but in practice, the keys are uncomfortable to hold in such a manner (as well as difficult to get into position quickly) and are unsecured, resulting in their twisting and pivoting upon contact with one's target. Twisting and pivoting of the unsecured keys can easily lacerate one's fingers, resulting in possible muscle and nerve damage. One's keys should never be used in this manner.

7. NAILFILE: Most metal nailfiles, although having a pointed tip and perhaps even a small handle, are far too flimsy to stab a person without bending or breaking. While it might be unpleasant to be jabbed with one, this flimsy weapon would only be effective versus the eye or throat.

8. BROKEN BOTTLE: The broken bottle is probably the improvised weapon most often brandished in various action-adventure films, and broken glass is considered to have one of the sharpest edges known to man, so most people reasonably assume that by simply busting off the end of a handy bottle they will instantly be armed...unfortunately, this is seldom the case. First, many bottles are extremely difficult to break—you can literally smash a bottle against the edge of a table several times with the only result being a chipped table; Second, the bottle could shatter in your hand, leaving you injured as well as weaponless; Third, you could easily catch a piece of broken glass in one of your eyes, impairing your ability to fight and possibly even resulting in irreparable blindness; and Finally, if you do succeed in breaking the bottle without injuring yourself, chances are that you will only be holding the bottle's neck with a little bit of jagged glass at the end—a weapon lacking in both range and intimidation value. If the only improvised weapon available to you is a bottle, I'd recommend leaving it intact for use

as a bludgeon, possibly smashing against your opponent for maximal damage. The bottles broken on television shows are specially designed to be broken in such a manner—usually by first selecting a specific type of glass bottle and then weakening it with a blowtorch—please do not attempt to replicate the falsehoods seen on television with the expectation that they will work in reality.

9. IMPROVISED "FLAMETHROWER": Not only has this fantasy weapon been featured in many action-adventure films, but it has also been endorsed by numerous underqualified "self-defense experts." Typically, an aerosol can filled with spray paint, hairspray, or WD-40 is sprayed across an open flame (usually from either a lighter or a burning cigarette), igniting the flammable droplets in an impressive fireball. Anyone touting this foolishness as "effective" is an imbecile. Not only are the droplets consumed instantly (resulting in minimal range and little chance of seriously burning an adversary), but there is a significant risk of the flame entering the cannister and detonating, engulfing the sprayer in flames and peppering him with shrapnel. NEVER ATTEMPT THIS!

10. WHISTLES AND ALARMS: A determined attacker will immediately snatch this away from you and smash it. It is unlikely to attract help, but is sure to piss off your attacker.

11. "YUCKY STUFF": "Ewww...stay away, or I'll wipe this on you!" Some emotionally stunted imbeciles seem to think that the threat of having sludge, slime, raw egg, pudding, rotting garbage, or a "dog turd on a stick" dirty the clothes of an attacker will actually make him reconsider targeting them; however, the far more likely result is that the attacker will instead pummel the naive fool into whimpering submission before gleefully force feeding him the substance in question. What worked on the schoolyard bully in 3rd grade will hardly faze a degenerate crackhead who wallows in squa-

lor. The only things in this category that possess any intimidation value at all are skunk lure and toxic waste.

12. APPEALING TO HIS BETTER NATURE: Goblins do not have morals, ethics, or mercy—if they spare you a beating, it is because they felt it was not in their best interests to waste their time administering one. Goblins are predators who perceive those weaker than themselves to be nothing more than mealtickets and playthings, and nothing you can say will alter this fact.

13. ASSERTIVENESS: If you haven't got anything to back up your cocky attitude, you could easily turn a simple mugging into a serious stomping—and you would probably deserve it. An offended predator will feel compelled to "put you in your place" through whatever means necessary, which will probably result in your being maimed or killed. Predators very much resent being condescended to or threatened by those they perceive as weaker than themselves, and will gladly take the extra time to hurt such a person even when it does not appear to be in their best interest to do so. Don't pretend to be a "tough guy" if you're not...you'll be fooling no-one but yourself.

14. SUBMISSIVENESS: The goblin might simply take what he wants (belongings, money, dignity, sexual release) and leave without stomping you into a coma, or he may choose otherwise. Some deviants would feel a thrill at the seemingly unlimited control they suddenly had over another human being and might decide to "make the most of it" (culminating in torture and murder), while others might loathe your pathetic weakness and decide to punish you. If you choose to go totally submissive, you are willingly permitting the goblin in question to decide your fate...do you feel he will act responsibly? Fight, flee, or negotiate, but *never* allow your future to depend solely on the whim of some degenerate criminal. If you are unable to make important decisions about your own

future, others will be happy to make them for you—usually being sure to take full advantage of your weakness.

ENDNOTE

This section was intended to be entertaining as well as informative. I truly hope that you will never actually need to pick up a tool to defend yourself with, but if such a situation should arise you are now empowered with the knowledge that one is never truly unarmed, and should now have a basic understanding of the strengths and weaknesses of various improvised weapons. Such knowledge will give you added confidence in your ability to protect yourself and others.

The Aftermath

WARNING!

The following essay is intended for entertainment purposes only! It would be highly illegal to violate the law by failing to report a homicide or attempting to dispose of a body! If you violate the law in such a manner, you could reasonably expect to be sentenced to life imprisonment! Always be a good citizen and obey the law!

Okay, you've successfully stopped an unlawful attack by means of lethal force, and now there's a body on the floor...what now? If the incident occurred on the street, and there were no witnesses, you could simply walk away—but if it occurred in your home or workplace, your problems are just beginning.

First and foremost, unless the top of the goblin's head is missing, and the contents of his brain pan have been sprayed across the room, be advised that *he might not really be dead!* That's right folks—he could be "playing possum," "faking it," or "lying in wait." The moment you get within grabbing range, he could stick a knife in your belly or empty a tiny .25 automatic into your face. Do *not* approach the fallen goblin! Don't think that nudging him with your boot will make him holler—research has shown that some wounded soldiers have remained silent and motionless even after having been bayoneted! If a gun is still in his hand, feel free to fire a round into the back of his head (just be sure not to do it at point blank range, or you might have a lot of explaining to do). There is a high probability that a gunshot or knife thrust into the back of the knee would result in a response from a conscious individual, but there is a slight chance that a doped up (or highly motivated) individual could ignore such mistreatment. If blood has

157

ceased pumping out of a deep wound, that is a reliable indicator that the heart has stopped beating.

Next, you need to collect yourself. The worst thing you could do at this point would be to dial 911 and start blubbering all sorts of potentially incriminating (or otherwise damaging) information into a tape recorder! After ascertaining that the fallen goblin is no longer a serious threat, make yourself a cup of tea. The familiar motions of making tea (or coffee, if you prefer), will relax you; and drinking the warm caffeinated beverage will give you energy for the task ahead. While you sit drinking your tea, calmly think about what you shall tell the police when they arrive. Think of what impact your words will have on a jury, as you can be certain that they will be written down (if not recorded—or even *videotaped*). Say something like, "He was going to kill me!" or "He didn't give me any other choice!" Be sure to let them know that you regret having killed a man (regardless of how you might *truly* feel)—"I didn't want to hurt him! I can't believe I actually killed a fellow human being! I feel *terrible* about this! I hope he doesn't have a wife and kids!" Think about how you're going to explain yourself—just be sure not to volunteer too much information or start "running at the mouth."

Once you've collected yourself, find your attorney's telephone number—*but don't call him quite yet!* If you don't have a lawyer on retainer (or one you've used in the past) who is qualified to handle criminal cases (and many lawyers will *refuse* such cases), pick a couple of good criminal attorneys out of the yellow pages, writing their numbers onto a scrap of paper which you can fold up and stow in your wallet. If the police become rude, accusatory, or start making you feel uncomfortable, you have the right to stop their questioning at any time, until you have a chance to consult with your attorney—and *"if you cannot afford an attorney, one shall be provided for you."*

In the event that your attacker is unarmed, you'll need to find him some sort of weapon—it'll look real bad to the jury if you killed an unarmed man, even if he happens to be three times your size, high on crack, and has a history of violent offenses. Do not deceive yourself into thinking that you'll be acquitted for homicide simply because you were rightfully defending yourself! People are unjustly convicted of crimes they didn't commit nearly every day. Several people I've known have secreted an old butcher knife (wiped free of prints and kept in a plastic bag) somewhere in their house expressly for this purpose, and it is not uncommon to hear of an urban policeman having a small untraceable "drop gun" hidden in an ankle rig if ever the need arises for him to "cover his ass." After taking the goblin's pulse at gunpoint (and finding none), repeatedly press the fingers of his right hand onto both sides of the blade (or slide) before placing it into his hand (if using a handgun for this purpose, ascertain that you've left no prints on the shells, clip, or inside the magazine well).

If an hour has passed, and no police have yet responded to the gunfire, you can get out the cleaning products. Be aware that blood will seep through carpeting and into cracks, making it nearly impossible to clean up all traces without tearing apart the floor; however, this is wholly unnecessary unless the police actually suspect you of having shot someone, are able to obtain a search warrant, and have the proper equipment to detect trace amounts of blood (Luminol spray, a blue laser, and special optics). If the goblin is lying on the carpet, you might want to wrap it in a tarp (or plastic tablecloth or dropcloth) before dragging it into the kitchen or bathroom. Using paper towels and old rags, try to soak up as much blood as you can before attempting to clean the mess up (all bloodstained paper towels, rags, and clothing must later be burned, or otherwise destroyed—just don't try to toss it in the garbage—especially *someone else's* garbage!). Even if your carpets are woven from polyester treated with a stain-repelling coating—*and* you happen to own a steam cleaner—there is still a high probability that a noticeable stain will remain. Plan on destroying the carpet (and sanding the floorboards underneath).

Once the contaminated area is as clean as it's going to get (expect to spend at least an hour blotting and scrubbing the stain on the carpet—*"Out, damned spot!"*), you're going to have to think about what you're going to do with the goblin. If you just leave him there, soon he'll start to stink up your house and attract flies.

Burial is usually a poor option. It is time consuming, attracts too much attention, and leaves a great deal of evidence for investigators to find. If you feel that you *must* bury the body, never attempt to do so on your own property—and *especially* not in your basement! There is a myth that caustic quicklime will accelerate decomposition, but it is untrue. Lime may partially mask the odor of rotting flesh, but it will react with the fatty tissues to mummify the body—thus *preserving* evidence that otherwise probably would've been destroyed!

Dumping in a body of water also tends to be a poor option (unless chained to an old anchor and sunk far out to sea). Bodies dropped into a river nearly always wash up downstream, lakes can be dragged with hooks for an unrelated case, divers could discover the body, or the gasses associated with decomposition could cause the body to bloat and bob to the surface. If you *must* dispose of the body in water, be sure to weight it down (chains work well for this) and stab deep into the lungs, stomach, and bowels to prevent bloating.

Many bodies have successfully been disposed of simply by rolling them up in the stained carpet and transporting it to the dump, but there are too many risks involved. For example, the junkman might remember what your car looked like (a rolled carpet on the roof is very conspicuous), and your hairs could be found by an evidence collection team (they use special vacuums for this type of work).

Burning a body takes an incredible amount of heat, leaves trace evidence behind, and smells horrendous. You would not want to attempt such an undertaking in your apartment's incinerator or your backyard burn barrel. If you choose to make a bonfire in a secluded area, you could draw a low of unwanted attention. An acetylene torch could be used to consume the flesh and soft tissues of a body, and could also be used to char the bones, after which the charred bones could easily be pulverized with a sledgehammer. The next rainstorm would eliminate most of the trace evidence.

Woodchippers and chainsaws shouldn't even be considered. Aside from being incredibly noisy and messy, the equipment will be impossible to clean afterwards, and will soon begin to smell really bad—imagine doing something like this with rented tools!

Dismemberment is probably the most efficient method of disposal. You'll have to detach yourself from what you're doing, or it could really screw you up emotionally—even some of the toughest criminals I've known would have difficulty cutting a warm human body into pieces. After several hours have passed, the blood will begin to thicken, and the task will be considerably less messy. A hacksaw could be used to remove the limbs and head from the torso (*don't* use an axe—it would be too easy to inadvertently injure yourself or damage the floor). If, for whatever reason, identification needed to be obscured (perhaps the assailant was someone who could easily be connected to you), the clothes should be removed (and later destroyed), after which the hands (along with any tattoos) could be burnt black with a blowtorch, and the teeth and face could be smashed with a mallet. Each piece could then be placed in a plastic trash bag for transport (I'd recommend double-bagging with Hefty "Cinch Saks"—use the 33 gallon size for the torso, and the 13 gallon size for individual parts). *BE SURE TO WEAR GLOVES WHEN HANDLING THE PLASTIC BAGS!!!* Disposable latex gloves are good, but long rubber kitchen gloves are far more durable. The limbs and head could then be placed in a suitcase, and the torso in a backpack. The hacksaw should be disposed of as well. Be sure to take a shower and put on some clean clothes before leaving the house!

The items could then be transported to a secluded area to be dumped. Be sure to *remove the parts from the bags* prior to dumping, as the bags will preserve evidence much longer than if they were exposed to the elements. You may wish to scatter the parts in different areas, but this is hardly necessary. The best place to dispose of the parts would be deep in the woods (perhaps far behind a rest area—at least half a mile). Other options might be to dump the parts down an abandoned mineshaft, a steep embankment, or a campsite privy. If it is too inconvenient for you to drive out into the wilderness, you could always toss the parts down a storm drain (although someone would probably see you doing so—even at 0300). The bloody plastic bags can be disposed of nearby. The hacksaw should be disposed of in a separate location—perhaps the river. The luggage can probably be reused (although you'll probably feel more comfortable getting rid of it sometime later).

After the body has been disposed of, you'll want to double-check your vehicle and home for evidence before retiring for the evening. Surprisingly, you might be ravenously hungry—just try to avoid dairy products or greasy foods which might not agree with your stomach. Take a long rest—you'll need it.

The next day, arrange to get a new carpet of similar color and style. Hopefully no blood was sprayed on the upholstery or wallpaper, as that'll make cleanup far more difficult. It is important to keep a clean house, and not only are bloodstains a bitch to get out, but they'll be a constant reminder of the unfortunate incident. The stains *must be eliminated!* Simply pulling the sofa over the spot on the carpet will not do.

Killing a man (even in self-defense) is hard enough for most people to handle—think about how difficult it would be to deal with dismembering the body and putting it in your luggage! Of course, not many people would have the stomach to do it. You'd have to accept that it was "you or him," and that you're doing the right thing—because if you called the cops you would surely be arrested for murder, and possibly even convicted—especially if the circumstances were "questionable," you used an unlicenced weapon, or you happen to have a criminal record. Do you really want to be front page news and hounded by morbid curiosity seekers? Do you really want to risk the possibility of losing your job, as well as your standing in the community, for being a "man of violence?" Do you really want to risk being separated from your friends and family, and thrown in a dank pit with a bunch of criminal deviants who'll try to turn you into a bitch? And for what? Because society says that we're required to inform the authorities when we kill someone who had the audacity to attack us in our own home? I think not! If I'm forced to kill someone in self-defense, ain't *no-one* gonna find out about it if I can help it!

And remember, *there's no statute of limitations on homicide!* That means you can never talk to anyone about what you have done (nor should you call up an associate for assistance). "Oh, but it wasn't murder—it was self-defense!" you might say. Sure it was, but do you think a jury would believe you after the prosecutor tells them how you deliberately chose to conceal the incident from authorities, and then proceeds to describe in graphic detail exactly how he believes you must've disposed of the body? They'll think you're a monster, and would be unlikely to pay attention to any evidence which might exonerate you. To avoid the stress associated with constantly worrying about such things, it is advised that you put the whole ugly incident out of your mind. *It never happened.* It is common for persons who've been through traumatic experiences to completely block out any recollection of the incident, and this appears to be a coping response which occurs naturally. As long as you don't keep dwelling on the incident, and there are no reminders about (bloodstains or "souvenirs"), this will be easier than you think.

Afterword

If you've only learned one thing from reading this book, I hope it's that *violence is not a game!* Popular culture (action movies, television shows, videogames, etc.) seems to actually *encourage* the use of casual violence as a means of settling disputes, but rarely shows the true end results (crippling and maiming injuries, hospitalization and physical therapy, infection and other "complications," lawsuits, prison, and criminal vendettas—sometimes people even die). Furthermore, movies and television often show us techniques that *will not work* in real life—it is a fantasy world created by people who have never experienced the things they are attempting to portray.

Self-defense is neither a game nor an "art." It is not intended to soothe damaged egos by putting others "in their place," nor is it meant to impress others through a childish display of *machismo*. No...it is a deadly serious matter, to be used only when one's life is imperiled and retreat is impossible. Remember, once you have committed yourself to an act of violence you will have to live with the consequences of that act *forever*...do not take these words lightly! Never kill if you only need to wound; never wound if you only need to hurt; and never hurt if you only need to speak the truth (or simply walk away).

I truly hope that you will never find yourself in a situation where the use of violence is unavoidable, but if this does occur at least you'll now be better equipped to deal with it.

About the Author

C. R. Jahn (AKA "Captain Hook") has been studying the fighting arts since the age of five, and is the Director of Righteous Warrior Temple, a literary and philosophical society dedicated to educating people about the Warrior Path. His website is at:

www.righteouswarriortemple.org

Other than that, not much is known about C. R. Jahn…and C. R. Jahn prefers to keep it that way.

0-595-21651-X

Made in the USA
Lexington, KY
06 March 2010